SELMA EVANS

HEALING YOUR INNER CHILD

A JOURNEY TOWARDS THE WOUNDED AND LONELY CHILD WITHIN YOU. LETTING GO OF THE PAST AND REGAINING EMOTIONAL STABILITY

ASIN: 979-12-81498-33-4

TABLE OF CONTENTS

INTRODUCTION

Are you struggling to let go of your past? Lost in a cycle of negative thoughts and behaviors? If so, you may be holding onto an inner child. An inner child, sometimes referred to as the wounded child, is a representation of the self that you've abandoned. It may show up as a debilitating fear, a negative reaction, an unhealthy relationship, or a deep wound.

The inner child is a survival mechanism that emerged to allow you to navigate the world as a kid. If you were subjected to any painful experiences as a child (abuse, neglect, abandonment), it is likely that you created an inner child as a way to survive those circumstances. It also may be created during periods of intense pain and trauma like physical or emotional illnesses, war, poverty, famine and natural disasters.

The wounded child may feel helpless, damaged, angry, sad, afraid and/or unworthy. It seeks negative experiences to validate its existence, feeling incomplete without the wounds. The wounded child typically seeks out power over others to feel good about itself.

The wounded child uses the same coping strategies during adulthood that it employed as a child to survive. It employs self-destructive behaviors like self-harm, addiction, eating disorders and sexual promiscuity. It will judge, criticize and blame others. It will hold on to the belief that it is not good enough, or may feel superior to others.

The wounded child can be a great survival mechanism in childhood but becomes destructive when it remains in the adult body. When your inner child becomes your primary identity, you are living life through a filter of victimhood and childhood wounds.

You can heal your inner child by allowing it to go. Let it loose, give it space and love. It will give you space and love back when you allow it to do so unconditionally.

You can heal your inner child by surrendering to the present moment. Stop trying to control the past or the future. Stop blaming others. Stop obsessing about mistakes or what-ifs. If you are in a situation that you feel is out of your control, take a deep breath, open yourself to all of life's possibilities and surrender to its unfolding.

You can heal your inner child by becoming whole again. You may be looking for the answers to what went wrong in your childhood but it is not necessary for you to know this, nor is it necessary for you to change the past. Let go of your need to know what happened and focus on accepting yourself for who you are now.

Acceptance is a pivotal part of healing from trauma. When you accept that you live in the present moment, you become completely present to your feelings and emotions as they arise. You can no longer be controlled by past experiences and wounds.

You can heal your inner child by practicing present-moment awareness, compassion and forgiveness. Actively suspend judgment of the wounded child whenever it appears in your mind. Be objectively curious about what happened to create the wounds and how those wounds led you to where you are today. Use compassionate curiosity to understand yourself. Use compassionate acceptance to accept the wounds without judgment. Use loving humility to let go of the need to be superior and worthy.

Accept your past and put it in perspective. It is a part of you, but it does not define you. You can release its hold on your life and move forward with love and compassion for yourself and others.

This book will guide you through a process of letting go of the inner child. You will be guided to identify the wounds that need to be healed. You will use visualization and creative writing exercises to heal them. Through creative expression, you can release energy from your past wounds and create space for positive experiences.

You can heal your inner child by simultaneously grieving the loss of your past. You will learn how to create a more authentic you while releasing the past. If you feel stuck in life, this healing process will help you move forward more easily.

This book is for everyone who has suffered trauma in their childhood or lives with an inner child that does not feel whole, happy or connected to themselves or others. It is a guide to healing from wounds and reclaiming your true self.

This book is for anyone who wishes to understand their emotions, behaviors and relationships better. It is designed to help people get in touch with the root of their pain and create a path to healing.

This book is also for anyone who wishes to change the way they react to stress, anxiety or fear. You will learn how to respond to your wounded child with compassion rather than fear, hatred or rage.

As you heal your inner child, be compassionate with yourself. You are still healing from something that happened to you as a child. Do not punish yourself for having survived. Do not punish your inner child for being who it is today. You must be kind to yourself and your inner child.

You can heal your inner child by learning to be happy about what you have today. You can release the need to be superior and worthy. You can turn your attention away from the past and focus on creating a life full of opportunities, joy, happiness and love for yourself. This will help you gain more control over your life, rather than letting the past determine who you are.

When you heal your inner child, you will be less reactive to dependency, fear and anger. As you heal, you will be able to better care for yourself and others. You will feel more secure, happy and whole.

To heal your inner child, you must accept the past. Acknowledge the past as a part of you but not something that defines you. You cannot change the past but you can create a new future for yourself. By learning to accept the past, you can stop making it so important in your life.

CHAPTER 1: SIGNS AND SYMPTOMS OF THE WOUNDED CHILD IN ADULTHOOD

I f you're reading this, chances are there is some area of your life where you feel like a child again. You may have childlike feelings of being scared, guilty, or not feeling secure. You may be experiencing behaviors that are childish in nature, including being overdramatic about things, being rebellious with no purposeful direction, or seeking attention at any cost. These are all common characteristics of a wounded inner child.

All of us have been wounded at some point in our lives, especially if we had toxic parents that emotionally or physically abused us. If this occurred, then it is very likely that you were cut off from your true self; your inner child.

The wounds caused by the dysfunctional family system may not be apparent until later in life when you encounter situations that trigger the pain of the past. You feel like a wounded child on the inside and act like one on the outside.

It is important to heal the inner child in order to move forward and regain your true self. The following are signs and symptoms of a wounded inner child:

1. Fear of Being Alone

This may be a reflection of what you experienced as a child. As a child, you were often alone and abandoned by those who were supposed to protect, guide, and love you unconditionally. This leads to trust issues because the child fears the world is not trustworthy.

2. Trying to Control Your Relationships

This could be your attempt to fix your wounds because deep down you feel like a victim. This is a dangerous way of being because you are controlling others instead of being in control of yourself.

3. Not Feeling Loved

If you were emotionally forsaken as a child, you may be carrying the pain of not being loved and accepted into adulthood.

4. Constantly Searching for Validation

You may constantly seek approval, attention, and acceptance because you didn't get enough of it as a child. You are unconsciously trying to prove that you are OK by getting more attention than what was given to you as a child. This is dangerous because you are seeking validation from others instead of loving yourself first.

5. Feeling Helpless

You may feel like a victim of life and like there is no way out. This is usually a result of feeling abandoned; abandoned by the family system or society, or abandoned by God. You might also feel like there is no way to escape your pain because your inner child feels helpless and worthless.

6. Feeling Guilty about Failure

You may feel guilty whenever you make a mistake due to the wounds that were created when you were growing up. When you feel like a failure, it's because you couldn't be perfect and live up to the unreasonable expectations of your parents.

7. Being Overly Dramatic

You may be overly dramatic about everything because you feel like it matters. You may take things too seriously or too lightly because you are not in touch with how you really feel.

8. Being Rebellious without Direction

You may be rebellious without direction due to what your parents taught you about how to live life. You may have no direction in life or no aspirations because the only thing that was instilled in you was that parents are your role models.

9. Frequent Mood Swings

You may experience mood swings because you are reacting to something instead of being proactive. This could be because your parents never disciplined you when you needed it.

10. Addiction or Obsession with Certain Things

You may be addicted to certain activities, substances, people, or places because they provide false relief from your inner child's pain. You may also be compulsive in your thoughts, behaviors, or actions because you are running away from your pain.

11. Feelings of Not Belonging

You may feel like you don't belong anywhere because you don't feel like the world is safe or secure.

12. Failure to Learn Lessons

You may fail to learn lessons in life and end up repeating the same mistakes over and over again due to feelings of being aban-doned or rejected by family members or society in general. You

may also fail to learn lessons because you are not hearing them
or you believe they don't apply to you.

CHAPTER 2: EMOTIONAL DISTRESS

There are many sources of emotional distress. These include personal losses, traumatic experiences, and the loss of a loved one. Some people are unable to release the pain from things that happened in their childhood. The emotions from those experiences can carry on into adulthood if they are not properly resolved. Many things can contribute to your emotional distress including your work environment, your financial situation or your relationships with others. Emotional distress is a complex issue that can have many causes. Here are just a few of the symptoms you might experience when you are dealing with this type of stress:

Anger

When someone experiences a loss, they can become much more irritable and angry. They could also have a hard time tolerating even the smallest inconveniences. The problem is that there are people use this anger as a way to avoid addressing their true feelings. This usually happens in men who are trying to deal with the loss of a loved one.

Many people also become angry when they are trying to deal with unresolved childhood issues. You might experience feelings of anger that you did not realize you had. This can come out in the form of irritability or even rage. Anger is actually one of the biggest symptoms of emotional distress. It is an indicator that your stress levels are getting out of control and you need to do something about it before this situation becomes worse.

Fear

Fear is one of the most common symptoms of emotional distress. This is especially true when you are trying to deal with past traumas. Fear can manifest as irrational or paranoid thoughts and you might become more fearful about certain things happen in your life.

It is not be possible to address all these fears at once, but it is important that you let go of them one by one. It is okay to be afraid, but you should try to understand why you are afraid. Once you understand that, it will become much easier for you to move on.

Fear can come out in a lot of different ways. Whatever form it takes, it can be very destructive. You might find your relationship becoming strained because you are starting to feel isolated from loved ones. It could also cause serious problems at work or home. If this fear is not addressed, then these other symptoms will not go away either.

Grief

In most cases, grief is a natural feeling that you have to accept. When the loss becomes severe however, it can become a symptom of emotional distress. You might feel a lot of guilt and self-blame even though you know that it was not your fault.

The inability to overcome grief can lead to depression and other serious medical problems. Once you accept the fact that it was not your fault, then this will help you move on with your life.

Guilt

The other main symptom of emotional distress is guilt. This can be a negative feeling of responsibility for something you did or did not do. The most common area where this happens is in the area of intimate relationships. You may feel a great deal of guilt when a loved one dies or when you break up with a loved one.

This type of guilt can come from unresolved childhood issues. This is especially true if you feel that you were somehow responsible for your parent's divorce despite the fact that you had nothing to do with it. In order for you to move on from this guilt, you have to accept that it was not your fault.

Hopelessness

Many people experience a great deal of hopelessness when they are dealing with emotional distress. This can lead to a feeling of helplessness and a general sense of not being able to do anything about it. When this happens, people often feel as if they can't even take care of themselves, let alone their children or loved ones.

This can lead to resentment in your relationships. At the same time, you could experience a major loss of self-esteem. This will cause your problems to get worse in most cases.

We often wait until things get really bad before we address them. But it is important that you talk with someone about your issues as soon as they start becoming severe.

Anxiety

When you are afraid of something, your body will experience a lot of stress. This causes many different symptoms including muscle aches and pains, headaches and even digestive disorders.

This anxiety can cause you to become very irritable and even angry with others. Not all anxiety is bad, but the more severe types often indicate that you need to take action before your problems get worse.

Depression

Depression is another symptom of emotional distress. This can arise when you are dealing with past traumatic events. It can happen when you experience something like an accident or an illness. It is also common if you are dealing with unresolved issues of intimacy as a child. This is especially true if your parents did not communicate well enough about their own emotions.

Depression can cause major problems in your health as well as your relationships. It is one of the most serious symptoms of emotional distress because it can also cause a significant decrease in your ability to function.

Irrational Thoughts

Irrational thoughts are common even if you do not have depression. When you are dealing with emotional distress, you will often find yourself having many of these thoughts. They could be about the outcome of an event or about someone else's actions or behavior.

They can cause problems in your relationships because you might always be looking at the other person in a negative way. These thoughts can get so bad that you might start to get paranoid. This can lead to many serious medical problems, even including suicide.

If you think something, it will eventually become reality. You should not ignore these thoughts because they could lead to serious medical problems if not dealt with correctly.

Emotional distress is frequently a side effect of unresolved childhood issues. If you did not deal with your emotional needs as a child, then you might find yourself becoming defensive and angry as an adult when you try to sort through those issues. This is particularly common when dealing with unresolved issues surrounding intimacy.

CHAPTER 3: THE DEEP ROOTS OF EMOTIONAL WOUNDS

Most adults know what it's like to experience deep-rooted trauma. Our childhood memories are filled with vivid experiences that can haunt us for years, even decades. The emotional scars can cause a person to make unhealthy decisions and take drastic actions. Often, these events are minor and fade over time.

But for some, the trauma is so severe that they can't move on. They are stuck in the pain. Trauma affects the deepest part of us, our inner child. When we are scared or hurt, it doesn't seem to matter if the pain lasts one second or one minute. It has an intensity that feels like it will never go away.

Childhood trauma is a deep-seated psychological issue that can manifest itself in many ways. The effects of this trauma on the individual may not be felt until adulthood. Childhood trauma can cause serious mental and emotional issues such as anxiety, depression, high levels of stress, and difficulties with relationships later on down the line.

Trauma can cause deep-seated feelings of weakness and lack of confidence. The person may not feel happy or free because they are not aware of their inner child's true potential. The inner child is an aspect of a person that is pure, innocent, full of energy, and creative. When this part of the individual has been damaged by trauma, it can be extremely difficult for them to heal.

The affected individual will also be unable to express the joys of life to others. They will have difficulty engaging in social situations because society demands that people act a certain way in order to be accepted. When the person has not healed their inner child, they may not feel comfortable enough with themselves to fully engage in social situations. Because it is based on personal feelings, this healing process tends to take much longer than others.

In order to heal, the person must become aware of who they are as an individual. They need to tap into their inner potential and learn to live from this place of freedom.

A way to do this is by coming into contact with one's emotions. This can be a very uncomfortable process, but it is necessary for healing to begin. By expressing the emotions that have been keeping the inner child from healing, the individual will begin to feel them as they truly are. Then, they can work through their feelings and heal on a deeper level.

This process can take years, but if one remains dedicated to the task, they can heal their inner child. The person will have to learn how to process the emotions that have kept them from being their true selves. The individual has to be willing and able to own up to all of the emotions inside of his or her body so that they can begin healing on a more fundamental level.

Emotions Experienced as Mistakes

In our childhood, we can be constantly bombarded with negative emotions such as fear, anxiety, regret, grief and guilt. Sometimes, when we step into adulthood, we seek to escape these emotions that are experienced as mistakes. By focusing on your job or school work and pushing these perceived mistakes to the background, you become disconnected from your feelings – and so does your inner child. Only when you begin to heal your inner child will you begin to see these mistakes as a part of your life, but it is going to be difficult at first, especially if you have been told that mistakes are a bad thing.

While you may have been told not to feel emotions, they are still constantly being felt deep within your soul. The process of healing your inner child means re-experiencing your childhood. Not only must you understand the mistakes that were made in the past, you must also understand the way these feelings were experienced as mistakes. You are also going to have to learn how to heal your inner child from the mistakes that have been made thus far.

You may have been taught that being angry, sad, or afraid were mistakes and should not be considered as a part of a child's life. You may believe that people should endure negative emotions without showing them to the rest of the world because it is embarrassing to show people you are human. It is this embarrassment that comes from showing your negative emotions that actually causes you to feel like they are mistakes. Because of this, you may have felt that the only way to get rid of your negative emotions is by not letting them exist.

To heal yourself from this, you must re-experience the fear of being ridiculed because this is what you felt in your childhood when you acted in a negative manner. To overcome these feelings, you must confront how people would treat you in the past when you acted in a similar manner. You must learn not to be afraid to express your true emotions. Show the world that you are not afraid to be seen as a human with feelings.

When you heal your inner child from these regrets, you will realize that things are going to be different from now on. You will no longer feel the need to hide or deal with your emotions. You begin to embrace the fact that feelings are a part of a human being. If you begin to embrace your feelings as something that is good, then you will also begin to feel that your mistakes are not bad. You will see the mistakes as steps towards becoming a better person, and will still let mistakes happen every now and then. It is this release of negative emotions that will allow you to see the mistakes as a part of your life instead a mistake that should be avoided at all cost.

Unresolved Issues of Abandonment

As a child, you may have been neglected by your parents as they pursued their own dreams or other matters. This abandonment may have come in the form of divorce, death, or lack of interest in you as an individual. The main idea is that your parents put their own needs before you which caused you to feel like they did not love you or care about what happened to you. This feeling of abandonment can lead to many unresolved emotions.

You may have the fear that your parents do not care about you because they left you alone. It is this fear that causes you to doubt their love for you. You may also be afraid of being abandoned by other people in your adult life, such as your partner or friends. Even just the fear of being alone can cause you to act in a manner that will make people leave you because it is too much for them. These events can make your life very difficult and you may feel undeserving of the love of others.

This fear of abandonment makes it difficult to move forward because it causes things to feel uncertain. You fear of being left behind by other people.

Instead of allowing this fear to consume you, you must face it by knowing that you are not alone. You do not have to earn the love of others in order to make them stay with you.

Your inner child has lost trust in others due to the abandonment by your parents. To heal yourself from this, you must confront these fears and accept that your parents' love for you is unconditional, and you do not need to act in a certain way in order to make people love you, or to prevent them from leaving. These are the things that you must see in order to heal your inner child from this fear.

Fear of Commitment/Avoiding Engagement

As a child, you may have felt abandoned by your parents or that they were never there for you. You begin to feel like life is too uncertain and that it is only natural to avoid commitment. You feel like you need to keep your distance from people because it is inevitable that they will leave you behind again.

The fear of commitment can make it difficult to maintain relationships because you feel like you do not want to be close to other people. You will keep pushing people away because this will allow you the emotional distance that you need.

When this happens, your partner or friends may feel they cannot trust or believe in you. This can cause them to act in a manner that will cause you to pull away all the more. Your fear of commitment makes it impossible for you to engage with them emotionally.

When you realize that you are afraid of commitment, you must face the fear to move on with life. You need to stop pushing people away and allow them to get close to you. Let go of the fears that keep people at a distance from you.

The way to heal yourself is through introspection. This means that you know that the fear exists without having to confront it directly. You must recognize that it is a fear without being afraid of confronting it. Have the confidence to confront this fear and eliminate it from your life so you can engage with others.

You will realize this fear is based on false assumptions, and this will allow you to stop pushing people away. This will help your partner or friends because the only way they can feel comfortable enough to get close to you is if they can see how much they mean to you.

CHAPTER 4: COMMON SYMPTOMS OF UNRESOLVED CHILDHOOD TRAUMA

U nwanted memories from childhood can haunt us in adulthood. Sometimes they manifest as a host of symptoms that have a significant impact on our lives, affecting our self-esteem, relationships, and mental health.

The following are common symptoms experienced by people who have been traumatized. They are often referred to as the symptoms of unresolved childhood trauma.

Flashbacks

Flashbacks occur when an experience from your past is triggered by something in the present moment. They can be triggered by sensory input such as sights, sounds, feelings or smells. Flashbacks typically occur around the same time every day and involve a sudden surge of memories that run together. You may feel as though you're going through a movie in your head or as though you're reliving an event over and over again. The memories may vary from person to person because our brains remember differently depending on our age at the time of the incident.

Unresponsiveness

If you display unhealthy or immature behaviors in the way you interact with others, it may be due to past trauma. Often these behaviors are so ingrained in our minds that we don't recognize them for what they are. Instead, we see them as normal. These warning signs indicate that something is wrong with us and that we need professional help to resolve our issue.

Abandonment Issues

Many of us have abandonment issues as a result of early childhood trauma. As children, we naturally look to adults for guidance and support, but when those adults aren't there or fail to meet our needs, we can become confused and frightened. We may withdraw into ourselves and develop an attitude that makes it difficult for us to form relationships later in life. Our abandonment issues can become so severe and so ingrained that we may exhibit self-sabotaging behavior such as self-mutilation, promiscuity, etc.

Overreacting

Whether it's a violent outburst or an emotional breakdown, our reactions to certain situations may seem amplified because of the emotional instability that unresolved trauma creates. You may feel that you're out of control and too emotional to handle any given situation. Feelings of anger, sorrow, confusion, frustration, etc., are all based on the traumatic experience you endured when you were young. These emotions can become so powerful that they overwhelm you.

Fears and Phobias

Many of us face fears and phobias that stem from childhood trauma. As children, we're constantly redefining what's safe and what's dangerous based on our experiences with the world around us. This can be especially true if we're raised in an environment where other people are abusive or neglectful, or if there were other traumatic influences, such as war, death, natural disasters, etc.

Self-Abuse

As children, we often don't have the tools to handle our emotions, so we may physically harm ourselves. Similarly, when we're adults, we may choose to self-harm as a way of avoiding our trauma and its accompanying emotions. The resulting physical and mental scars can be very painful and difficult to deal with.

Toxic Relationships

Some of us may struggle to form healthy connections with others as a result of childhood trauma. Because we haven't learned how to trust others, we may find it difficult to develop healthy relationships due to the shame and shame-based behavior that arises from unresolved trauma. It can also cause us to feel as though others are to blame for our feelings, which can lead to anger and hostility.

Self-Medication

Some of us may use drugs or alcohol in order to self-medicate when we feel overwhelmed. Addiction is often a symptom of unresolved trauma because it can help us forget our pain temporarily. Unfortunately, this method of calming the mind doesn't work in the long run because your brain adapts to it and it becomes harder to stop. Many drugs cause problems in the long term because they're addictive. This is why it's important to seek professional help when you're trying to overcome an addiction.

Self-Doubt

As children, we may not have learned how to understand or manage our own emotions. Therefore, we may experience self-doubt, which can cause us to question our own worth and value. This can stem from trauma in your childhood or it can be triggered by the self-esteem issues that many of us struggle with in adulthood.

Anxiety and Panic Disorders

Anxiety disorders are often symptoms of childhood trauma. Perhaps we've witnessed someone being hurt or killed, which makes us angry. Or perhaps our early training led us to worry about all the things that could go wrong in our own lives. The result is an anxiety disorder, which makes it difficult for us to function normally in society because we have difficulty living in the present moment.

Manipulative Behavior

Some of us may use manipulative behavior as a way of dealing with unresolved trauma. We may become angry or upset, and then take it out on others in order to express our pain and discomfort. Some people resort to manipulation to avoid their own issues, but others use it as a way of getting what they want.

The Overbearing Parent

The overbearing parent is someone who has high expectations of their child in school, at home, and in society. They put pressure on their children to excel at everything they do and to be perfect all the time. The overbearing parent is extremely critical of their child and constantly finds fault in what they say and do. They often tell the child what they should do, rather than asking them what they want to do. The parents tend to make all the decisions for the child, rather than allowing the child to make their own choices. These parents tend to dominate the child or take over their life. They often make the child feel insignificant and/or powerless.

The overbearing parent can have a tremendously negative impact on the child's life. They may interfere with every part of the child's behavior, including friendships and other relationships. The child may feel like they're not able to do anything without consulting the parent first, which can lead to the child becoming overly reliant on their guidance.

The parent may praise or flatter the child incessantly, even when they know that they've done something wrong. They might cover for the child's mistakes or convince themselves that the child couldn't have possibly done anything wrong. The child learns to believe in their own infallibility because it's what they have always been told.

The overbearing parent will also make the child feel guilty at every turn. The child may get punished for things they didn't do, while others are allowed to get away with behavior that would get them punished in a normal scenario. This can be felt by the child for years because of how ingrained it is in their brain, and will only lead to more difficulties down the road.

Overly strict parenting can also cause major behavioral problems in children. They may experience frequent tantrums, which are usually fueled by fear. They won't be able to express themselves distinctly because they're scared of the consequences that are attached to their actions. If they do something wrong, they'll be punished for it immediately, rather than being allowed to learn from their mistakes.

The child may grow up avoiding physical contact because the parent makes them feel uncomfortable when they hug, kiss, or touch them. They'll also be extremely self-conscious around their parent, so they won't be able to express themselves as freely as they could with a normal adult. The child will also feel inferior compared to their parent, which can lead to a long-term inferiority complex.

The overbearing parent may also place unrealistic demands on their child. For example, they might want them to attend an Ivy League college or pursue a specific profession when the child isn't interested in those things at all. They might also be overly critical of the child's friends and their behavior. If one friend does something wrong, they'll accuse the child of having bad friends rather than looking into the issue further.

The parent may also force the child to take activities that they're not passionate about, such as sports. They may also be unrealistic in what they expect them to achieve through school or work. They're likely to want their child to make a lot of money and to succeed in a specific profession despite them wanting to pursue a different career.

The overbearing parent can also create an environment that's hostile to creativity, which can make it difficult for the child to pursue their own interests. This is especially problematic because the child will almost always aim to please the parent. If they don't, they may be punished or criticized for it. They will never be allowed to take any risks or do anything that could possibly get them in trouble, even if it's something they're interested in.

This kind of parent will also project their own insecurities onto the child. They may have a very hard time accepting that they have flaws or that they can't do everything perfectly. The child may feel like they're never good enough, even if they're doing exactly what the parent expected them to do.

The overly controlling parent will also force their child into a rigid routine that's designed to make them feel comfortable and secure. They want them to know where they're going to sleep, eat, and play but won't allow them to deviate from it at all. This is because they don't trust the child, even when they know that their child is capable of making good decisions. The parent doesn't want their child to stray from the plan they laid out for them, which can lead to serious consequences in the future.

The Self-Sabotaging Parent

Self-sabotaging parents are the people who continually sabotage their own efforts to be good parents. They may know that they should be doing something different, but because of fear and shame, they choose to do the same things over and over again, despite the damage this causes. They may not even realize what they are doing. This behavior must be addressed so the family can heal.

One of the most common traits of the self-sabotaging parents is never letting their children see them as anything but perfect and infallible, and as such, they never hear anything negative about themselves from them. Children can never say things like, "You're not doing this right," or "You're hurting me," or "You're yelling too much," or anything else negative directed at their parent.

As a result, when they become adults, these children are often completely shocked to discover that their parents are in fact human beings who are "not perfect" at all. They often find this realization extremely traumatic. They blame themselves for their parents' shortcomings and inadequacies. They feel that no matter what they do, they will never be able to live up to people's expectations of them, and therefore, they may become very anxious or depressed about the failures of their own lives.

Self-sabotaging parents often feel guilty and embarrassed about their mistakes and will often try to cover them up, which only makes the problem worse. They refuse to take responsibility for what they do and instead blame others or circumstances for their actions. They also find themselves unconsciously compelled to repeat their own mistakes, which only makes things worse. As a result, self-sabotaging parents tend to repeat the same destructive patterns over and over again.

The most important thing to remember about self-sabotaging parents is that they are doing the best they can. They are commonly acting out of their own feelings of guilt, shame, resentment, anger, or fear. If you get angry at them or trying to change your self-sabotaging parent's behavior, you are only making the problem worse.

Most of the time, self-sabotaging parents are unaware of how their behavior affects their children. They often do not understand why they feel the way they do or what their behavior has actually done to further damage the relationship.

If you are the self-sabotaging parent, it is important to understand that your behaviors are affecting your relationship with your child(ren). The only way you can change is to accept yourself completely for who you are and to deal with your fears, insecurities, guilt, shame, or anger.

Self-sabotaging parents need acceptance and compassion before any substantial change can occur. If you are the child of a self-sabotaging parent, the best thing you can do is to learn how to give him or her this kind of acceptance. Rigid family rules and conditional love are usually the results of a parent who needs unconditional love. They are often very afraid of being abandoned or criticized by their children.

Abuse by a Parent or Sibling

You may have been living in a dysfunctional family where the overriding theme was neglect. In this type of environment, you felt less love and more physical and emotional pain. Perhaps you were hurt by a parent or sibling who had the power to make decisions for you. They may have been mean to you, hit you, pushed you around, or not cared about your feelings at all. You felt alone and unloved. Your family environment was like a closed box, with no way out.

If your early life was not healthy, it can be hard for you to trust the people in your life when you become an adult. The early losses and neglect can leave deep wounds inside you. This may result in problems with self-esteem and self-confidence.

The emotional pain of neglect may also lead to poor impulse control. The child learns not to feel true feelings because the parent will not tolerate them. As an adult, you may become so numb, with so little sense of your own needs that you don't know what is real, or how to take care of yourself. You may want strong feelings but fear them at the same time, and live in a constant state of anxiety or anger. You may not have a sense of identity or may feel that your needs are all based upon what others want or need. You are living in the past, reliving things that happened when you were young.

If your parents were too busy with their own problems to care for you when you were a child, then the emotional pain may be even greater. You felt neglected and alone, but you didn't know how to make it better.

In order to feel safe in your world, you have to have a healthy foundation of trust or a safe base. In the context of the development of attachment, all children need a base from which they can explore their environment with safety and confidence. As adults, if we want to feel safe, we must heal that child who learned that he or she is not safe in this world. This requires that you have the courage to face the past with an open heart, face your feelings with honesty, and commit yourself to being with them. In this process, you need empathetic witnesses who can help you understand your pain and experience your feelings.

In order to heal from the inside out, you must be ready to feel your fear, rage, and sadness. If you are not ready to experience these feelings then you will not be able to close the distance that separates a child from their emotionally unavailable parent or caregiver. You must be willing to take time to be with your feelings. Previously, you were unable to take this time and as a result, your feelings were not attended to.

It is important to remember that not all bad parents are abusive. Some parents are emotionally unavailable due to their own pain and wounds from childhood abuse. These parents may become abusive or neglectful because they can't get close to others. In this case, it is helpful for the parent or caregiver to support their child's healing. Since the parent is the one who can best ensure that the child will grow up feeling safe in this world, it is important that they heal their own wounds and come to terms with issues from their past.

As an adult, you carry a lot of fear and anxiety about the past. If your parents were emotionally unavailable or punitive, you may have felt that life was a fearful place and that you were not safe in this world. The emotional pain of neglect will increase the intensity of your inner child's fear. You may seek out relationships where you feel safe for some time but will always leave because the person will not be able to give you what you need.

CHAPTER 5: 10 INNER CHILD ARCHETYPES

Archetypes are the psychological foundations for how we experience life. They are the ingredients that make up our experience of life and how we interpret our experiences. Archetypes can appear in many different forms, from small parts of a character's personality to a whole persona. You might think of an archetype as a persona or character that you see in yourself, and it might be the reason you have certain beliefs or emotions about something.

The following are hypothetical inner child archetypes that you might want to consider. As you read each one, ask yourself if it resonates with your own inner child.

1. The Rescuer

Your inner child might be a Rescuer if...

- When you were growing up, you felt like it was your responsibility to look after your family. You were the oldest child, so you felt like it was your job to take care of everyone else in the family. You were always doing things for other people and taking care of them.

- The majority of your childhood was spent looking after the people in your family and taking care of everyone else, including yourself. Your inner child feels responsible for everyone else and wants to look after them as best as it can.

2. The Caregiver

Your inner child might be a Caregiver if...

- You always feel like you're looking after others, even though it's not really your job. You might take on the responsibilities of someone in your family. You also feel like it's your job to look after people in your life, even if they don't need help.

- You take on other people's responsibilities and spend time looking after them instead of outing yourself first. "Poor little me" thoughts are typical for Caregivers who feel guilty when taking care of themselves.

3. The Rebel

Your inner child might be a Rebel if...

- When you were growing up, you might have gotten in trouble a lot. You often acted out when things weren't going the way you wanted them to. You might have gotten into huge arguments with your parents because of your anger issues.

- You're still angry about things that happened in your childhood, but you don't remember why or how it happened. Your inner child might act out or be angry with someone in your life, because you were angry with someone in your childhood.

4. The Lost Child

Your inner child might be a Lost Child if...

- You do not remember certain aspects of your childhood. You might have memories of things that happened when you were really young, but not much of what happened afterwards.

- You can't even remember how old you were when certain events happened or what happened during specific moments in your life. Your memories of your childhood are fragmented and incomplete. You feel like it's really important to find out what happened to you, because you feel like it's the only way to get closure.

5. The Trickster

Your inner child might be a Trickster if...

- When you were growing up, you might have gotten into trouble for doing things to get other people in trouble. You liked to make jokes about serious things that were happening in your life. Your idea of "fun" was creating problems for others.

- You make jokes about serious things in your life for laughs, because you're going through some kind of existential crisis. You find some situations funny because of how absurd they are, but not because you actually find them funny. You don't really mean to cause trouble or get anyone else in trouble, but you still do it.

6. The Wounded Child

Your inner child might be a Wounded Child if...

- You feel like you've been through a lot in your life, but you don't want to talk about it with the people in your life. You prefer to keep things inside and suffer on your own. Sometimes you might get really lonely, but you can't find anyone who understands these feelings that are affecting you.

- You keep certain aspects of your childhood to yourself

and ignore others entirely. You feel like you're going through a lot of pain, but you don't want to talk about. It's hard for you to trust anyone because of things that happened in your childhood. You might feel worthless or abandoned by everyone, because your parents didn't take care of the emotional problems that they created for you.

7. The Helpless Child

Your inner child might be a Helpless Child if...

- When you were growing up, you felt like nothing could be done to make things better. You thought that there was something wrong with you, and that no one could understand what you were going through.

- You had experiences in your childhood that left you feeling hopeless and unable to cope. You find certain situations really hard to handle, because you don't have the tools or skills to do so. You don't have enough con-fidence in yourself to take action in certain situations.

8. The Hero

Your inner child might be a Hero if...

- There were people in your life who you really looked up to when you were growing up. You always wanted to please these people in your life, so you tried really hard at sports or other activities, even though they weren't really for you.

- You look for people in your life who can make you into a better person. You also feel like it's your job to help people out who are less fortunate than you, because your parents didn't take care of the problems they created for you.

9. The Partner

Your inner child might be a Partner if...

- You weren't really close to your parents when you were growing up because they weren't really there for you. Your best friend was probably someone who wasn't in your family.

- You like to be in relationships with others, because you like to make people happy. You don't do what you need to do in order to make yourself happy, because you don't think it's important.

10. The Performer

Your inner child might be a Performer if...

- When you were growing up, other people tried to

pressure you into performing for them. They wanted you to play sports, perform in the school play or other activities, and other things that made other people happy. You didn't really want to do these activities because they weren't really a good fit for your personality. The expectations of others made you feel confused and pressured into being something that wasn't really authentic to who you are as a person.

- You take pride in the things you do for other people in your life, even if you're not really proud of yourself. You exhibit certain behaviors that make other people happy, but don't really enjoy them.

CHAPTER 6: EXPLORING THE INNER CHILD WITHIN INTERPERSONAL CONNECTIONS

Your inner child has a huge impact on your relationships with yourself and others. Here are some examples of how your inner child can affect the way you relate to other people:

If you have a Wounded Child as your inner child you will always feel lonely. You will usually go through periods where you don't even want to be around other people. You may consider other people worthless and incapable of understanding the problems you're going through.

If you have a Wounded Child as your inner child, you might be very hard on yourself for not doing enough things in your life.

You might feel like everyone else is really good at doing things, but you're the only one who doesn't know how to do these things.

If you have a Wounded Child as your inner child, you might think that certain problems are really hard to solve. These problems will feel impossible to overcome, because other people aren't taking the time to help you. You might feel like your life is no longer worth living, because it feels like no one cares about the issues that are affecting your life.

If you have a Wounded Child as your inner child, you will feel like there's something wrong with you. You might think that you're worthless, even though other people tell you that they love you. Your self-worth will feel really low to you, and this low self-worth is what makes it hard for you to maintain relationships with other people.

If you have an Abandoned Child as your inner child you'll probably always be searching for someone who can fulfill the role of your parent. If you don't have a real parent as your role model, you'll probably try to fill the empty space as best as you can. You'll probably use other people as tools for getting what you want out of life, and won't really care about how they feel. This might lead to a lot of arguments with both yourself and others.

If you have an Abandoned Child as your inner child, you'll probably be very lonely. You might long for the days when you had your family around, but realize that those days are gone forever. You'll probably become jealous of other people who still have their families, and feel like it's impossible to ever reach the point where you're happy with yourself.

If you have an Abandoned Child as your inner child, you tend to push the people who care about you away. You might feel like it's too much of a hassle to listen to what other people have to say, because you don't want to deal with the pressure that they're putting on you. You might not want to deal with the stress of caring about someone else, because it reminds you of how much you really care about the issues in your life.

If you have an Abandoned Child as your inner child, you will usually be alone. You don't really want other people in your life. You will probably slander other people for not trying hard enough to understand you.

If you have a Lost Child as your inner child, you might scatter your energy in too many different directions. You will probably be greedy when it comes to love, money, happiness, and all of the things that make life worth living. You might want to try to be everything for everyone in your life.

If you have a Lost Child as your inner child, you'll always feel lost. You'll feel like everyone else is really good at making decisions, because they're not afraid of what's going on in their lives. You will probably feel like you don't have a clue when it comes to making your own decisions, because you don't really know what you want out of life. You'll probably feel confused about how life works, and this is going to make it hard for you to build a healthy relationship with yourself.

If you have a Lost Child as your inner child, you'll always feel different from everyone else. You might feel like no one understands the reason why you're feeling so lost, because other people don't understand that you're just a child. You'll probably always feel like you're not good enough to participate in activities with other people, because you fear other people will mock you for not understanding how life works.

If you have an Innocent Child as your inner child, you'll want to be treated as if your actions never hurt anyone. You'll probably try to prove to other people that you weren't responsible for anything bad that happened in your life. You might even contradict the way people are telling the story about your life, because you want to be viewed as innocent.

If you have an Innocent Child as your inner child, you might think that it's everyone else's fault that you're not doing well in life. You'll probably feel confused and angry about what's going on in your life, because you feel like you don't have any control over how things are going.

If you have an Innocent Child as your inner child, you'll need someone to tell you that everything is going to be okay. You might feel like other people don't actually care about the issues that are affecting your life. You'll feel like your life is totally worthless if you don't have a family member around to take care of you.

These childhood wounds create a negative self-image in your mind, and this negative self-image is what sustains your victimhood.

If you continue to believe a victim is a part of who you are, you'll be unable to break the cycle, because you'll continue doing things that don't work for you.

In order to break the cycle, you must start working on your inner child issues from the inside out. You must start working on your issues around abandonment and loss, and feel free of any emotions associated with them. You must learn how to recognize and deal with these feelings so that they don't affect who you are as a whole.

If you can handle these things, you'll start having fun with your life again You'll start to appreciate people that care about you, and ignore people who would normally bug you. You'll learn to make a choice between what's fun and what's not fun, and then just enjoy life for what it is.

If you can handle these things, then you will become free. You will be able to stop believing in all of the negative content you used to believe in, and will start believing in yourself instead.

CHAPTER 7: THE WOUNDED CHILD WITHIN YOU

You need to heal your inner child because it is the source of all fear, fear that prevents you from experiencing and enjoying your life. If you could look at your past as just a story, the pain cannot touch you anymore because there is no reality beyond the story. You can change and improve without feeling or manifesting fear, anxiety, jealousy, or any other emotion that keeps you from being free and happy.

When you are aware of the inner child within you, your awareness expands to include its deep wounds and scars from past experiences. You become aware of how these wounds have been affecting every aspect of your life. It is this awareness that is essential for change and healing.

The journey of healing can be slow and challenging at times, but you move forward when you realize the value in healing yourself. It is like taking an uncomfortable step towards your true self, which you want to be within this lifetime. Instead of avoiding the pain, you are willing to live through it. By accepting your inner child's unpleasant experiences, you are able to release the pain that keeps you trapped in your past.

Becoming aware of and recognizing your inner child you will result in the healing that is needed. Then the pain cannot hurt you. You are now free to live your life as if it is the most beautiful story ever told.

The blocks are cleared, the family patterns are gone, and your desire to live your life fully manifests.

When we bring awareness to our pre-conscious programming we find that we may be holding on to pain and suffering from the past. The more we understand that these painful feelings are powerless in the NOW, at the moment, at this moment, in this NOW. They only have the power that you give them.

The key to the healing process is not about removing particular events or feelings from your past, but rather, bringing that pain into this moment and allowing it to move through you without getting caught in it.

Your inner child must be nurtured. When you are hurt by others, you feel angry and upset. Instead of fighting the emotions that are causing you to feel angry, it is more helpful to notice that they are here and allow them to move through you.

When you become aware of the pain in your inner child's past, you can easily see that whatever happened in the past is not happening now. One of the challenges for most people is that they have been trained to believe what happened in the past will affect their lives in the present.

In order for your inner child to be whole and healthy again, it is important to release emotions, thoughts, and feelings related to traumatic events in the past. To heal your inner child, you need to let go of painful self-judgments that are holding you back in the present moment.

It is crucial to be able to let go of painful memories in order to experience your true self. When painful memories are re-experienced by the mind, attention gets focused on the negative feelings instead of being in the here and now where all good things are found.

It is only when you are fully focused on the here and now that positive thinking can take place. Only when you are in the moment, experiencing the moment, do you become aware of all the opportunities available to you.

When you are lost in painful memories, thoughts, and feelings from the past, it makes it difficult to accept who you are right now. When your attention is brought back to who you are in this moment, then your true potential will be discovered.

Negative thinking can make you believe that who you are in the present is not good enough. When you focus on what is not working in your life, what you are doing now has little significance.

Your task is to be fully present. Something new will always come into your life if it is meant to be. By being fully in the moment you create the space for something new to happen.

The pattern can be changed when you realize that what happened in your past does not have to be your present or future. You can change your old beliefs about yourself, about others, about what is acceptable, and learn to think differently.

When you are in this state of allowing, forgiveness can occur naturally. This is not an act of will but of allowing yourself to feel what you need to feel without judging or censoring it. This state of allowing is also called "non-resistance" or surrendering.

When you surrender to what is, you are no longer resisting the moment. You are then open to receiving guidance, support, and love. This is the true nature of life.

When you are fully present, letting go is not a conscious decision, but something that comes from deep within the core of your being. When you have been doing this for a while you develop what I call "piercing" abilities. This means you can simply allow anything to happen without judgment. You only need to accept it and let go. When you surrender, you begin to let go of all your fears and resistance. While surrendering, you become aware that there is much love and support available to you and much love within you.

If we don't face our fears and heal our inner child, we keep repeating the patterns of pain and hurt over and over again. Healing means becoming aware of the patterns in your life so you can release them unconditionally. You must heal your inner child without any expectations or demands otherwise it will not work. Unconditional release is the only way to heal your inner child.

You can be whole and healthy when you understand that your past does not have to control you. You are now free to love, learn, and grow as a human being. You can create a life full of meaning and purpose instead of focusing on what feels bad from the past. When you hold on to pain from the past, it will become a barrier to love in your present.

The Hurt Child Still Resides Inside of You

One of the most painful aspects of childhood is the hurt that comes from being unloved or rejected by parents or caregivers. These hurts are usually buried so deep in our psyches that we can't even tell they are there. They become a part of who we are, although we may not be aware of the fact that they are ever-present.

The result is an inner child who is fighting for survival against a whole system – the family – which has turned its back on him. It's no wonder these children grow into adults who have little sense of self-worth. No matter what they achieve or how high they rise, they feel as if something is missing from their lives.

As adults, we may even feel that we are failures, that life has somehow cheated us. We look around at our world of material affluence and wonder why we can't find happiness. We think that love and success will finally bring us a sense of peace, but happiness always seems to be out of reach.

Whatever our circumstances, we feel as if we're on a treadmill going nowhere.

The loneliness of the Hurt Child deepens as he looks for love in all the wrong places. He chooses partners who are unavailable or abusive, or who neglect or exploit him. He may become involved with alcohol or drugs to try and fill the emptiness within him.

This is a dangerous path. It can result in a life of self-destruction, mental illness, and violence. In the worst cases, this pain drives the individual to join a cult or become an evil person who harms people in their own way.

The Hurt Child's childhood is a time of great betrayal. The child feels as if he or she has been stripped of everything – loved for who they are – and left with nothing. This feeling is made even worse because the adult world doesn't seem to understand what has happened. In fact, the adult world may blame the child for his problems.

The pain from our childhood wounds can lead to a lifetime of destructive behavior. However, if we are aware of the wounds and their cause, we can begin to heal our inner child.

To heal the wounds that our inner child suffered, we need to recognize them for what they are once and for all. This might be the hardest step because the hurt can surface so suddenly and unexpectedly. It can be frightening to discover how vulnerable we were as children. But to heal, we must face up to these memories rather than avoid them.

This is not an easy task because it involves accepting responsibility for past choices made under force or duress. And it is hard to confront these painful memories when we feel alone and abandoned. But if we listen to the inner voice of the Hurt Child, he can tell us what he needs from us.

Healing the inner child is a courageous undertaking. To heal, we need to open our hearts and share our hurts with others. We need to be willing to hear what he has to say and reassure him that we want the best for him. And we need to take steps in our own lives to reconnect with him and heal the wounds that he felt at such a young age.

This can be difficult because many of these wounds were inflicted on us by people we loved and trusted. But they were human beings who may have had their own problems and difficulties. They may not have known how to help or protect us, but that doesn't mean they didn't care.

We must remember that the hurts we suffered as children are real. We must not deny them or blame ourselves for what happened to us. Instead, we must let our hearts be open to the Hurt Child still residing within us.

The Scared Child Within You

Often, when people think about the inner child, they think of an innocent and playful youngster. This is not always the case. For some children, this inner child can be wounded or scared. They are too timid to speak up for themselves when they need help because something has happened in their life that made them feel powerless – maybe abuse or abandonment or neglect. These children can feel powerless and ultimately, that life is not worth living. They become stuck in their own wounded inner child, unable to express themselves fully and not knowing how to communicate effectively with others. It is as though they have no voice. The fears that the inner child represent are very real. They are the fears created by some childhood trauma. The child may have become afraid of people, places, or things. They may feel safer when they are alone because they do not have to face the world around them. This fear can exist in many adults who were neglected or abused when they were young.

You may identify with a Scared Child if you:

-have a fear of people or places that seem completely irrational

-fear abandonment at the hands of people you love

-feel trapped by fears from your past

-are afraid to express your true self because you are too scared of rejection or humiliation

-have a fear of failure and/or inadequacy

The Scared Child is an inflamed inner child that is even more vulnerable than an average child. By being afraid of everything, this child has turned itself off to the world. When you are able to get in touch with this child, you will see the pain and grief it is really feeling. This child needs special love and care. It can be protected from its fears if it understands that these fears are not real, but rather things that happened in the past that will not hurt it again.

The scared child is afraid of people, because it believes they are not good to them. It has no one to turn to when it needs help or comfort. It was wounded and abandoned by its parents. The scared child's mind works differently than the average child's –

a very protective system is created in order to protect itself from all of life's overwhelming stressors. It is as though this child has built a wall around itself so as to not have to experience the pain of the past. The scared child is afraid of love because it has been hurt before by those who said that they loved them. The scared child is afraid that it will be hurt again. It is going to need a lot of therapy and a great deal of nurturing in order to overcome its fear and take a chance on love again.

The scared child has become stuck in its own fearful mind. When you are able to connect with this inner child, it is possible for you to see the pain it feels inside. You will discover that it really misses having a loving parent to protect it from all of life's stresses. It feels alone in the world because it has not learned how to trust others. It is their inner child that holds these fears.

The scared child needs love and attention in order to heal its wounds and begin to trust others once again. Those who love the Scared Child will need to be very patient. They will need to be consistent in order for the Scared Child's doubts and fears to begin to subside.

The Scared Child can learn from the past and protect itself in the future. The Scared Child must learn that it is safe in the world. It must learn that it is safe to love others again.

The Angry Child Has Taken Control

If the Angry Child has control, it can be because you have not yet identified the cause of your anger and learned how to control it. It is very common for an Angry Child to take over. If you think about the typical stages of development, it makes sense. When you are a small child, you feel safe in your mother's arms. But when things go wrong – you fall down and hurt yourself or a sibling pushes you off a swing – the world can suddenly seem unsafe and unfair.

The Angry Child has power because you have not yet learned to take the power into your own hands. You have not yet learned that it is okay to feel anger.

If you are not taught that it is okay for your inner child to feel angry, the Angry Child will take over and try to handle life's problems by lashing out verbally and physically at yourself and others.

In this way, the Angry Child takes your power away from you and gives it to anger. The more he gets angry, the more power he has over you. And the more power he has over you, the less safe you feel.

He may also take your power away from yourself. If anger is a coping skill that allows him to handle life, then your Angry Child will use it as a defense against feeling hurt by events in life. Over time, you may begin to lose faith in yourself. You may begin to believe that your feelings are bad. You may even begin to tell yourself that others are right when they criticize your behavior.

If you listen to the Angry Child, he will tell you that everything and everyone is bad. He will tell you that anger protects you from being hurt or letting others hurt you. He will tell you that anger helps you get what he wants – that it gives him power over the world around him.

To heal your Angry Child, you need to learn that anger is a normal reaction to hurt. You need to learn that your feelings are okay and that it is okay for you to feel them. You have to learn how to control anger instead of letting it control you.

If you let the Angry Child get angry at everything, you will feel hopeless about the world and yourself. But once you begin to believe that it is okay to feel angry (and that your feelings are okay), the world will seem like a safe place again. You will think of yourself as a worthwhile, valuable person.

When you stop identifying with the Angry Child and start to see that it is okay to have feelings of anger, then the Angry Child will be forced out of your life. In its place will come a healthy sense of self-worth and a conviction that you can make things happen in life. Once you understand that your childlike anger is not bad, and then you will be able to control it so that it will not control you.

The Busy Child Has Occupied You

The Busy Child is a master manipulator, convincing you that you have no time for anything other than work and other responsibilities. He tells you it's too much effort to make time to take care of yourself. The Busy Child prevents you from taking the time to be creative, play, or have fun. He tells you that taking time to do the things you love is selfish. The Busy Child is very convincing, but it's all a lie. You will never be able to live the life you truly want to live if you allow this child to control your every action. He keeps you locked in a vicious cycle of overworking yourself, which leaves you feeling overwhelmed and stressed, which in turn makes it impossible for us to make time for ourselves. Most of all, it prevents us from taking care of our health. By allowing the Busy Child to rule our lives, we are missing out on so much. The Busy Child keeps us from creating art, playing music, exercising, watching our favorite movies, reading books, and so much more. If you can't take care of your health, you won't be able to live your dream life. You may even get sick or hurt yourself because of stress or exhaustion.

The Busy Child doesn't care if you're happy or sad, healthy or sick. He only cares about doing things for himself. You have let him consume your whole life, and he will continue to grow more powerful if you don't take steps to stop him from controlling your life.

The Busy Child has kept you in a cycle of overworking for so long that you have likely already forgotten what it feels like to live in the present moment. Life is happening in the here and now, but you're always in the future or in the past. Your thoughts are focused on stress, getting to your next task, or making sure that everything gets done on time. You can't live your dream life because your dreams are lost somewhere in the real world. They haven't been able to find some home in your busy mind, and you can't find a way to bring them into reality.

You need to free yourself from the Busy Child so you can discover who you really are. Once you regain control of your life, you will discover that there is so much more to life than work and deadlines. You will have the time and energy essential to live the life that is calling out from deep inside your soul.

In order to reclaim your life from the Busy Child, you need to slow down. You need to take time out to relax and enjoy the pleasures of life. Spend some time taking care of your physical, mental, and spiritual health. If you don't take the time to be present in the moment, you will never know exactly what you want out of life. Being present allows you to be more creative and to see opportunities that are right in front of you. It also helps you identify your true passions, which is key to creating the life that is truly meant for you.

Once you slow down and take control of your life, you will never again let the Busy Child dictate your every action. You will stop overworking and allow yourself to have fun. You will be able to work less and create more. You will begin living on purpose rather than on autopilot. By recognizing the Busy Child for what he is and freeing yourself from his control, you can make a life full of purpose and passion.

The Caretaking Child Within You

You may think of a Caretaking Child as the "inner parent" in your psyche. This is the child from your past who took care of you and now you are taking care of it.

The Caretaking Child is the part of you that is always looking for security and direction and gets you into "parenting" yourself or other people. It feels the need to please others, to take care of things, to hold on to what's familiar, or to always be in control. Or it may be the part of you that feels like a victim and is always waiting for someone else to take care of you and provide security. The Caretaking Child uses fear as a way to motivate you and protect you from danger – even when there is no danger – so it helps you to focus on what is safe or familiar or controllable, rather than facing change or uncertainty.

This inner child within you believes that if something bad happens, it's your fault, and therefore if something good happens, it's also your doing. The Caretaking Child uses fear to motivate you, but it can also hold you back because you want to avoid the fear that is associated with change or the unknown.

The Caretaking Child is an extremely powerful part of you, but it can also be your greatest obstacle. It wants what's best for you, but wants to control every detail in order to keep you safe and secure. The Caretaking Child can be very controlling because it wants to be in charge. The more scared the child feels, the more controlling it becomes.

The Caretaking Child in you will resist change that doesn't feel safe or familiar, and often resists taking risks that may involve getting hurt. The child from your past sees change as a threat to security and tries to hold on to what's familiar. The more you resist change, the more your Caretaking Child will try to control you and find ways of making it safe again.

To deal with your Caretaking Child, you have to understand that this child in you is not the real you. It's part of your psyche, but it's not who you are.

When you stop believing that this child in you is the real you, then you can start to let go of it. As long as you are identifying with it and letting it control your life, you will never be able to experience your full potential. But when the child in you stops being so important, you can start to feel what's right for yourself instead of letting your past take over, making decisions based on what's familiar or safe rather than what's best for you.

When the real you starts to emerge, you begin to feel a sense of safety and a feeling of letting go. You start to sense that taking risks might be okay because if things do go wrong, it's not the end of the world. You feel more able to take some chances without worrying about the negative consequences because you aren't so afraid anymore. You start to trust in yourself and what's possible in your life.

When you let go of the Caretaking Child and stop running from the fear it creates, this child in you will start to let go of its controlling and restrictive ways. It will start to feel more relaxed and will start to accept that it's okay for things to change. The inner child in you will also stop trying to take over everything and control your life because it will realize that you can't fix everything, and that life doesn't revolve around fixing the past.

The inner child in you wants to be free of the past too and will start to let go of the barriers it once created to hold on to what's familiar or safe. This will help you to move forward rather than staying stuck in your life.

The inner child in you will let go of the need to control; it will let go of fear and will start trusting in your ability to handle the situations of your life.

When the inner child in you starts to let go of fear, it will also help you to realize that when people are in your life, they are there for a reason. They are not in your life merely because you need them or because you were attached to them in the past. People come in your life for many reasons and when the time comes, they will no longer be there for a reason too. This may not be easy to accept at first, but you can't keep people in your life who aren't meant to be there.

When you understand that people will come and go, and they will leave their own personal mark on you, you can let them go when they're ready to leave. You understand they're not in your life just for comfort, protection or security. They're meant to help you develop and grow into the person you are destined to be.

CHAPTER 8: REDISCOVER THE CONNECTION WITH YOUR INNER CHILD

As adults, we are often so busy living our lives that we forget to take time for ourselves. We put work first, family second, and often neglect our own happiness. But once you have found the time to reconnect with your inner child, there are many ways that you can start making yourself happy again.

We also often feel guilty about having fun. We feel like we should be putting in extra hours at the office, or maybe studying harder. This guilt creates a distance between us and our inner child.

When you are able to reconnect with your inner child, you will be able to let go of this guilt. Then you will be able to enjoy your time with friends and family, or take some time out for yourself. It doesn't matter how busy your life is or how many hours you work, everyone needs some time for themselves every now and again.

One of the main ways that we can reconnect with our inner child is by finding ways to play. Because we live in a grown-up world, many of us have forgotten how to play. But it's not too hard to figure out. Find some place where you can be alone and free from distractions, then find something that makes you feel like a kid again. It could be blowing bubbles, going on a swing, or anything else that brings back that sense of fun.

Connect with your inner child by watching cartoons or playing some simple games. This doesn't need to be anything too serious, just something that will help you to forget about the real world for a few minutes. Sometimes, it can be hard to find time to play. But if you are able to push yourself, you will soon learn that it is essential. Your inner child should be treated with respect and made sure that they always have time for themselves. This will also allow them to flourish and become the best version of themselves possible.

Another way to reconnect with your inner child is by finding ways to make yourself laugh. You used to laugh all the time as a kid, but now you may find it difficult to find even one thing that makes you giggle. This is because of all the pressure that you feel on your shoulders. You worry about everything from your job performance to your family's happiness. But when you are able to lighten up just a little bit, you will begin feeling happier about yourself and others around you.

If you need help finding ways to make yourself laugh, look for any comedy shows that you can watch or try to find some funny Internet memes. Go out and do something silly, like taking a selfie and posting it on Instagram with a filter so it looks like you are an octogenarian. The whole point here is to not be so serious and give yourself room to find at least one thing that will make you feel happy and relaxed.

Another way that you can reconnect with your inner child is by having fun with your friends and family. Spend some time with your family, be silly with your friends, or create new memories with them that will help you remember how you used to feel. You don't need to do all of these things at once, but keep an awareness of how your relationships affect your state of mind.

Try making time for yourself even when you're at work. Do something that you enjoy doing and take a break from everyone around you. You will be surprised how much more content you will feel once you have made the effort to reconnect with your inner child.

Whether it is taking a walk or having an online game with your friends, make sure that you take the time to disconnect from the rest of the world.

Remember, it's not about what you do to make yourself happy, but how happy you make yourself. So once you have reconnected with the fun that your inner child has, don't forget to give yourself a little treat as well. After all, that's what a child does for themselves. Sometimes it's so good to be a kid again for just a little while.

By reconnecting with your inner child, you will be able to improve your outlook on life. You will be able to reconnect with yourself so you can continue moving forward in your life, regardless of how much work is piling up.

The Healing Power of Love

As you probably already know, the love you experienced as a child is what made you feel accepted, happy and safe growing up. Your caregivers' love was crucial for your emotional development. When it's unconditional and comes with compassion, care, and respect for you as a person, love will do wonders for your psyche.

As a child, you craved unconditional love from your caregivers. You felt safe with those who accepted you as you were. No matter what you did, they would never reject you. Because of this, you felt completely accepted as an individual. They would always be there for you, listening to your thoughts, desires, and feelings.

At times, you did stupid things. You made mistakes. You didn't get everything right. But this love still held you in its arms to let you know that you were still accepted.

This kind of love during your formative years helps tremendously with the development of your identity. It enables you to explore who you are without fear of being criticized or punished for being different from others.

It's no wonder you had major issues if that love was not there, or if it was distorted. The lack or abuse of this love prevented you from knowing your true self, creating traumatic experiences in your past. As you now learn to love and appreciate yourself and others again, you're also healing the past and rediscovering your inner child.

When you acknowledge this part of yourself, understand its needs, and learn how to communicate with it, you can heal deeply. You can listen to your inner child that was silenced during childhood and show it that you love it unconditionally. That will set the tone for a new relationship with this part of yourself so that both will thrive in harmony.

For this process to take place, you need to really love yourself. You need to accept yourself, the good and the bad parts of yourself. Even when you make mistakes, know that you're human and forgive yourself. This is a very powerful way of accepting your past with all its good and bad, in order for it not to affect your present or future.

Love yourself, your challenges, your mistakes, and be there for yourself. Remember, you are never too young or too old to practice healthy self-love. When you feel ready and truly want this for yourself, you will start to see the results.

By loving yourself completely, you can heal your past and grow into a better person. There's nothing more powerful than the love that comes from within, to get rid of the sorrow and trauma that holds you back from living a happy life.

Play Therapy for the Inner Child

When was the last time you felt safe, relaxed, and at peace? If it has been for a while then it is likely that your inner child needs some healing. The inner child holds our memories of being loved and happy. When these happy memories are replaced with other memories, it can have a negative impact on who we are as adults. This is where Play Therapy can help. Play Therapy can bring back those happy memories that will allow the inner child to heal and to grow.

Play Therapy is a form of psychotherapy that aims to bring out an inner child's playfulness and creativity. It does this by using toys, art, music, drama, and crafts as a vehicle for self-expression. To truly experience Play Therapy you will need to find a qualified Play Therapist and book an appointment.

Play therapy is a process of exploring the inner child's thoughts, feelings, behavior, and actions. It can also be used to resolve disputes between parents and children or to understand the child's feelings about parents who are dying or divorced.

Play Therapy can be used to help the adult reclaim their childhood through memories, emotions, and imagination. Adult children of parents whose marriages were tumultuous may benefit from Play Therapy with the goal of working through unresolved issues. Play Therapy is also often an effective way of releasing hurt and anger, thus helping the person work toward feelings of forgiveness.

Play Therapy can also be effective in helping one work through some deep-seated fears. By using the techniques of Play Therapy it can be easier to uncover some of these fears that are still lurking in the unconscious. This can be helpful when trying to overcome some of one's more irrational fears.

Play Therapy enables an individual to truly get in touch with their inner child. The inner child can be very sensitive and easily bruised. This sensitivity is why it's so important to keep the child happy and healthy. Play Therapy can help you work towards feeling fulfilled by reconnecting with your inner child.

During Play Therapy, the individual will be asked to create a setting that is familiar to them. This can be done by playing with dolls, teddy bears, crayons, blocks, or any other toys that are appropriate for their age range. They can be asked to write a story about how the toys, objects, and characters relate to them. This story will help them connect with their inner child. They can then begin a dialogue with the characters that were created. The reason that Play Therapy is considered effective is that it brings out creativity, emotions, and imagination. It also helps the individual understand themselves in a deeper way. Once you understand yourself it will be easier to take care of yourself.

The individual can also be asked to distinguish between feeling and emotion. The feeling is when you have a strong emotional connection with something, such as anger, happiness, sadness, or fear. Emotion is when you have a more intellectual or rational connection with something, such as being angry over something that has occurred in the past that had some type of negative consequence.

It is important for the therapist to make sure that the person understands they are not just playing at their childhood, but that they are bringing it to life. This type of play will hopefully help them resolve conflicts that were created during their childhood and move forward into the present.

By working with these issues in a safe environment, the adult can move on with their life and experience healing.

Find a Way to Express Your Feelings

Before healing your inner child, you need to be able to express your emotions without fear of judgment or criticism from those around you. In order to do that, you must learn to tolerate the presence of even the most difficult feelings. Spend time with those who love and support you as well as those who cause discomfort and frustration by challenging your views. Find ways to practice self-compassion each day, no matter how hard it is to face painful emotions at first. When you feel the pressure of self-judgment, do not judge yourself as a bad person. Acknowledge that you are human and that no one is perfect. With practice, it will become easier to be more generous with yourself as you learn to embrace the good and the bad in your life.

It takes time to heal your inner child. Remember, you can take as long as you need to get over the past and move forward. One of the best ways to show how you are feeling is through drawing or other artistic expressions. What you draw doesn't have to make sense, but it can be a healing tool. For instance, if you drew a picture of being beaten up, and being tied down, then talked about it with a friend, you might realize that this happened to you. It will help you work through your feelings and begin the healing process.

You can also choose to express your feelings through music, dance, or other forms of nonverbal communication. These nonverbal forms of expression can help you get in touch with your feelings. For example, if you feel angry, you might dance for five minutes to the song "Gangsta's Paradise" by Coolio. If you are sad, you might dance to "Don't Worry Be Happy" by Bobby McFerrin. Or maybe the song that helps you express your emotions is a light pop number with a catchy chorus that may help you remember how it feels to move on from a painful experience.

You may also choose to write a journal entry about the events that have caused you pain. Tell yourself that you have been through tough times, and this is how it feels to get through them. Write about who you were as a child and how this event has changed you. If you find it difficult to talk with someone about your inner feelings, you might want to try journaling. With practice, this will become easier over time.

Many people find that writing helps them express themselves. Sometimes it is easier to express feelings on paper than it is to speak. For example, some people find it easier to write out their feelings through poetry than talking about what they are feeling. You can use poetry or other forms of creative writing to work through the pain and turmoil of the past.

Working with a counselor is also another way to help you begin the healing process. A counselor can help you to see how your life has been adversely affected by growing up in an abusive environment. They can remind you that you were not at fault and can help you to understand why your self-worth and self-esteem are so low. Many counselors use art therapy and talk therapy to help their clients work through feelings and heal from trauma and painful events of the past.

Expressing your feelings can be particularly helpful when you feel anxious, angry, or depressed. If you allow the world to know the truth about your past, it may help you heal and grow. It is okay to let others know your thoughts, regardless of how they may judge or criticize you. They may be surprised that you are not the person they thought you were, but that is okay. You don't have to hide your feelings with false expressions of happiness.

To heal your inner child, remember that you are the only person who can truly provide the healing he or she needs. Once you are able to express your emotions, it will help the healing process tremendously.

Draw a Picture of Your Inner Child

Everyone has an inner child. It's often the part of yourself that is pure, innocent, and free to dream without worry or anxiety. However, when you experience trauma or other difficult experiences in life, this innocent little kid in your mind becomes wounded and scared.

To help you connect with your inner child, I'd like to invite you to draw a picture of him or her. You can do this with crayons or markers, or if you're more of an artist, feel free to grab some paints. Either way is fine. Just put your favorite colors on paper and draw a picture that symbolizes your inner child. Hopefully, it will be something beautiful that makes you smile when you look at it.

Now that you have this picture, spend some time with it. Try to imagine your inner child in your mind's eye. What are their favorite toys? What are their favorite games?

Think about how it feels to look at them. Do you love them? Do they love you back? Can they feel your love or is that something they don't have the ability to feel yet? Maybe there is a part of you that still has wounds from being hurt in the past. You can play with these thoughts if you'd like or leave them aside for now.

Paint or draw another picture of your inner child and hang it up somewhere you'll see it often. Look at their innocent face; see how beautiful they are. Imagine if you could protect and nurture them and bring them joy and love throughout their whole life. How would that be?

Now that you're starting to see the child within you, what does he or she need? What can you do to nurture him? If your inner child represents the hurt, scared, innocent part of yourself, how can you comfort him and show him that everything is okay now?

It's important to realize that your inner child is not just with you now, he lives inside of you. You are his home, his place of security. He's the one who's always there for you, who knows all your cares and fears, and stands watch over you.

If you want to nurture your inner child, think about how he connects with others and how he feels when someone supports him and loves him. Think about how he deals with conflict and criticism and consider what support he needs from you.

Sometimes healing your inner child means dealing with the trauma they've experienced in their life. Other times, their wounds are too deep to heal and they will never come back to the person they were at their core. But don't give up on them! If their wounds are too deep, you can still love them even though they may not fully love you back. You can still nurture and protect them and help them heal into the most beautiful version of themselves.

The goal of this exercise is to help you know who your inner child is, what he or she looks like, and how it feels to be connected to him. Whenever you see your picture, see it as a reminder of who this child is and how much you love him. The power of this simple exercise is that you'll never have to forget about your inner child...he'll always be a part of who you are. This is a lifelong commitment, so keep drawing pictures of your inner child and keep working on strengthening your bond with him. If you take the time to care for him and love him, he will reward you a thousand-fold.

Working to nurture your inner child may seem daunting because there are so many hurt parts of them that need care. But each day is a new opportunity to show love to the young child within you who has been lost and hurt for so long. Don't pass this beautiful child by...he's the one who brings you the greatest joy! I hope this exercise helps you.

After you draw your picture of your inner child, take a minute to write about your experience. What did it make you think about? How did it make you feel? Do you need to do anything differently in your life to give your inner child better care?

Please remember to check in with yourself! The main goal of this exercise is not to make you feel worse...it's a reminder that there is a part of you that is still wounded and needs care. The goal of this exercise is to help you work towards being the guardian angel for your inner child, someone who can bring them healing, comfort, and joy.

CHAPTER 9: STRENGTHENING THE BOND WITH YOUR INNER CHILD THROUGH HYPNOTHERAPY

When under hypnosis, you are in a very deep state of relaxation. This is why some individuals find it so hard to remember what happened while they were hypnotized.

Hypnotherapy can be used to help you build a positive relationship with your inner child and empower yourself on conscious levels. Hypnotherapy can also be done during sessions with a therapist or psychologist who is trained in the use of hypnosis for this purpose.

All hypnosis is self-hypnosis. No one can make you do anything that makes you feel uncomfortable while you are under hypnosis. Hypnosis is considered a natural state of mind, and there is no possession or monster inside of your mind waiting to take over control of your body! It's just you.

Your inner child communicates with you through your imagination, emotions and memories. Your imagination gives images to your creative intelligence, which gives them the power to affect your emotions and feelings in the present moment.

When you are under hypnosis, there is less separation between your conscious self and your inner child. This is why it can feel like your inner child is more real than the adult you. Your inner child will use any opportunity to get its needs met, which can sometimes be embarrassing! It will sometimes express its emotions in ways that are not appropriate for the situation. It will also sometimes be angry with you for what it considers to be your neglect or maltreatment of it in the past.

Your inner child may also want to talk about details of your past that you are not comfortable talking about. You will have to learn how to listen to your child with love, patience and compassion. If you are concerned about what it is saying, you can always ask the therapist or hypnotist you are working with for their support.

You can work on these issues with your inner child by learning how to use the following techniques:

1) Conversations

Use your imagination to see your inner child in your mind's eye. The more you practice seeing him, the more real he becomes. Practice talking to him with love and compassion.

To make this possible, you must become willing to work on this process while under hypnosis. When you feel the relaxation come over you, begin by welcoming him into your mind's eye. Ask him how he is doing. He answers you by saying, "I am fine". Then you can ask him if he wants something. He answers you by saying, "Yes, I do!" You must be willing to listen to his answers and allow him to tell you what he needs.

2) Children's Games

You can play games with your inner child that will put him at ease. For example: He could pretend to be the youngest child in the family who has just come home after being away all day at school. He is excited to tell you about what he did during the day.

You could begin by imagining his excitement at coming home. Then you could imagine playing the part of a parent listening to your child with interest and love. You can remember how it felt to be a child and have someone listen to you with interest and love while telling them about your day.

3) Give Him a Voice in Your Life

Your inner child may not have had a chance to grow up because you weren't able to do so when he was younger. He may not even have had the opportunity to go through the experiences that all children do. He may not have had a chance to learn many of the skills that you did, such as playing sports, becoming an expert in a field, and so on.

So acknowledge that your inner child may be limiting himself to what he knows at this time.

4) Emotional Healing

Children feel emotions, but they don't understand them very well. They cannot fully express them on conscious or adult levels. Also, children who are neglected or abused sometimes do not learn how to process their emotions at all. So it is important for you to help your inner child learn how to express his feelings more effectively and with less suffering for himself and others. This can be done during hypnosis, when you will speak to your inner child on adult levels of consciousness.

Preparing For a Hypnosis Session

Before a hypnosis session begins, you will be asked to agree not to discuss the content of the session. You may also be asked to take off your watch or other jewelry. You will likely be asked to remove your glasses or contact lenses if you wear them. If you are afraid of darkness, it is good to take along a night light in order to avoid feeling uneasy during the relaxation period.

Before starting a hypnosis session, think about what you would like to accomplish during that session. If you are experiencing problems in your life, ask the hypnotist for suggestions that will help you solve them. For example, when you are having problems with anger, it may be helpful to have the therapist put you into a trance and suggest to you that all of your anger is gone. If there are other problems in your life that are troubling you, mention them to the therapist. Hoping for a good outcome is an essential part of the process.

Try not to worry about entering a trance while you are in the session. Asking yourself questions such as, "How will I know when I'm in a trance?" or "How can I tell if it was successful?" can keep your mind from being fully receptive to suggestions. Once you have these kinds of questions in your mind when you are being hypnotized, they will keep you from being able to listen to suggestions. The ideal condition for a successful session is a state in which the patient is relaxed and willing to listen carefully. As you relax, your mind will become open to the suggestions the hypnotist gives you.

If you become worried that you may not respond to the session well, it is okay to talk about this with your hypnotist. The therapist will be able to provide reassurance and advice for making the process more effective. If your hypnotist sees that you are becoming tense or agitated, he or she may ask whether there is anything wrong. If there is, remember that it is okay to talk about it. Talking about your fears can help you relax.

When the hypnotist puts you into a trance, he or she may insert suggestions immediately. If this happens, it is best to accept them and go with the flow. If you feel like they are not what you want, tell the therapist. He or she will then be able to give suggestions that are more effective for you.

Hypnosis is not a magic trick or an illusion. It is just an altered state of consciousness with the ability to reawaken your memory.

During hypnosis, there is often a period of deep relaxation or even complete sleep. You will go into this relaxed state by following the voice of your hypnotist. When he or she suggests it, you should let go and sink deeper into trance. After the session, it is okay to ask what you were asked to do while in trance. Your hypnotist can tell you about these suggestions and what results they produced. When you discuss the experience with the therapist, it will help you understand what happened. Talking about your experience can often help you remember what was said during the session.

Take a few minutes daily to write out the suggestions that your hypnotist gave you. By allowing them to sink deeper into your subconscious mind instead of forgetting them, they will become more embedded there and will begin to produce changes in your life.

CHAPTER 10: EMBRACE AND NOURISH YOUR INNER CHILD

I f you find yourself feeling unimportant or unneeded, it's time to take the initiative and show up again. Whenever we feel unseen, unheard, or unappreciated, we become invisible and withdraw into ourselves. To heal our inner child, we must show up for ourselves first before showing up for others. It's time for you to show up again.

Become your own best friend

As we heal, we begin to realize the importance of choosing our friends carefully. We begin to do more and more of what we want because our self-love has grown so much, and the love we give ourselves is flowing back to us tenfold. We feel stronger, lighter, and brighter because of our newfound love for ourselves. We begin to show up for ourselves and give ourselves time and space to grow and heal. We become our own best friend.

Become your own cheerleader

When we find the inner strength to place importance on ourselves, we start to feel empowered once again. We may begin to withdraw from the company of people who don't hold our self-worth in high esteem. Our inner child feels nurtured and loved, so we begin placing less importance on others' opinions of us. We stop seeking the approval of others because we know that they are not our primary source of validation. We cheer ourselves on, no matter what. If you are feeling invisible or ignored by others, it may be time to start showing up for yourself again.

Every action is self-affirming

As we heal, we recognize how everything in our life is a reflection of ourselves. Every action has an impact on how we feel about ourselves, and every word or phrase comes through us with great meaning. Every action is a way for us to communicate who we are.

When you feel unimportant and unneeded, it's time for you to take the initiative and show up again. The more you withdraw from others in order to protect your heart, the less likely anyone will be able to see you and give you the love and attention that you desire.

Begin to take action again

Often, we may stop doing things because we are not sure how to proceed, it's time for you to start taking action again. You can find yourself withdrawing from the company of others because you are not sure what to say or do. But it's time for you to start putting yourself out there and taking action in the world again. Even if you're not sure exactly how to proceed, challenge yourself to take the first step, and trust that the path will soon become clear.

Every action is a choice

The more we take action in our lives, the more we begin to feel seen and valued. The more you are willing to show up for others, the more likely others will show up for you too.

Every thought and feeling is a reflection of our true self

Sometimes, we choose to withdraw from others in order to protect our heart and to avoid the pain of rejection. We may hide behind masks and play small in order not to be seen or heard by others. Whenever we find ourselves feeling unseen and unimportant, it's time for us to begin showing up again for ourselves.

Become an initiator

When you start to feel invisible, it may be time for you to become the initiator. If you don't initiate conversation with others, they can't see that you exist. When someone constantly ignores us, we need to take the initiative and show up for them. If they are ignoring us, it may give us insight into how we treat ourselves all day long.

The more self-compassion we have for ourselves, the more likely others will feel safe around us too. We can initiate conversation with someone to show them how we really exist, but always make sure to approach them from a place of respect and love.

Become a model for others

If you show up for yourself first, others will soon follow. If you begin doing things that make you happy, the people around you will notice your happiness and will begin to emulate it. Become a model for others by being the best version of yourself each day. If you show up for yourself first, others will soon follow.

To heal your inner child, it's time for you to show up and take back your power and space in the world once again. Set boundaries and be assertive with others to ensure you are not being taken advantage of or victimized. Do things that make you feel happy and loved.

The more self-care you give to yourself, the less likely others will take advantage of you. We become our own best friend again when we take the time to love and nurture ourselves each day. Take time to be alone with yourself again. Reconnect with your inner child by having fun again. If you spend time with people who are constantly criticizing you or telling you that you are not enough, it's time to withdraw from their company.

When we spend time alone, we can reconnect with our inner child and rekindle our love for ourselves. It's your turn to give yourself the love that you deserve.

CHAPTER 11: RECONNECT WITH YOUR INNER CHILD THROUGH THE ACHIEVEMENT OF LIFE OBJECTIVES

In our childhood, we were taught what is important to us. We developed a sense of who we are and our place in the world. To heal our inner child, we must identify what is important to us as an adult. This can become overwhelming because it takes courage to find out what really matters to us instead of just doing things for others. We must be very willing to take risks and action so we can discover what is important to us.

Even though we may not remember most of the events that shaped us in our childhood, we most likely learned a lot by listening to and observing what was most important to our parents. By following and taking care of the things they wanted, we started to learn what really mattered to them. We can do the same thing in our adult life by staying true to ourselves and fulfilling the life goals that are most important to us.

It can be difficult to discover what is truly important to us as adults, but we can do so by listening to our intuition.

We should not feel pressured by society to choose a career that other people dictate that we should have. We should take time alone with ourselves, and then do what feels right for our inner child. Nothing is wrong with pursuing our own dreams, so long as it's safe for us to do so. We should not feel as though we have to live out the life goals of others.

We do not need permission to make decisions for ourselves, so long as it does not endanger others unnecessarily. We may think that certain life goals are not available for us, but if we believe deeply enough in them, they will show up for us at some point in time.

Another way to discover what really matters most to us as adults is by listening to the people closest to us. If we can identify what's important to them, we can be inspired by them and explore other possibilities that may be available to us. We have a wide range of possibilities out there unless we have closed ourselves off from them prematurely.

We cannot discover what is important to us as adults if we choose not to take risks and chances. We can either wait for others to empower us or we can take the initiative and do it ourselves. If we don't trust our own intuition, we will always be searching for approval from others.

Many of us have been conditioned by society that certain careers are unavailable for us. We worry that our life goals will never change for the better. We may even believe that we don't have a future or a purpose to live out.

One of the reasons parents may have been overprotective of us as children was because they thought that we were incapable of taking care of ourselves. They wanted to protect us from the world around us because they loved us so much.

As adults, we can continue carrying this belief with us, unless we learn how to discover what is truly important to us. We don't have to live up to the life goals of society if we don't want to. We can learn how to follow our own goals instead.

Once we become aware of what is important to us, we must take action and fulfill our life goals on our own. If we wait for others, we will never get around to it. We may even believe that taking care of ourselves is wrong or selfish. This couldn't be further from the truth. What is more important than taking care of ourselves first, so that we can then help others?

Many of us have sacrificed our lives to help others for many years. We may have done this because we felt guilty about what happened to our inner child. But we know on some level that just taking care of others is not enough for us. We must be willing to look at what really matters to us, and become aware of what is most important.

It's time that we take the initiative in our adult life. If we can become aware of what is truly important to us, then we can work on fulfilling our inner child's life goals.

Give Yourself the Things You Wish Others Had Given You in Childhood

As adults, we must take the initiative in looking after ourselves and fulfilling our inner child's needs. Often times, we take care of others before we take care of ourselves.

This is often because we had to take care of our inner child first as children. It was necessary for us to do so, because overprotective parents overburdened us with responsibilities that were not meant for us at a young age.

We often feel as though we have to do everything for others, as if we can't be happy unless others are. In reality, we have to be happy with ourselves first. All of our happiness lies within us. If we cannot accept and love ourselves, then we will never stop sacrificing our happiness for others.

We have been conditioned to believe that we have to live up to other people's expectations instead of our own. However, it is a myth that we must care for others first before we can take care of ourselves. This myth is a result of the overburdening effect of an overprotective parent, who loves us so much that they cannot trust us with anything at all.

Once we learn how to take better care of ourselves as adults, we can take good care of others as well

For many of us, it's time to take good care of ourselves for the first time. We must realize that there is nothing wrong with indulging our own needs and desires. We can love and care for others and take good care of them and still take great care of ourselves at the same time. We can allow ourselves to be happy before we take care of others. We do not have to sacrifice our own happiness for the sake of other people, even if they are family members.

Create Loving Affirmations for Your Inner Child

Finding ways to acknowledge and heal your inner child's emotional wounds restores the relationship between you and your inner child. This can create a deeper sense of self-love. Here are some affirmations to start you on this journey:

My inner child is a treasured part of me.

My inner child is worthy of being loved unconditionally by my adult self.

I have within my reach all I need to feel safe, secure, and in control in this world.

I have the power to heal my inner child by being kind to myself.

I can heal my child through unconditional love.

My inner child is just as important as the other parts of me.

My wise inner child has helped me accomplish great things in life.

I am grateful for my inner child and in knowing them, I become wiser and in touch with my true self.

My inner child is my guardian angel who guides me in making choices.

My inner child is not to blame for the things I did when I was a child.

I can forgive myself freely for what I did as a child.

I acknowledge the power of my inner child and its role in guiding me through life.

I love and accept myself unconditionally, no matter how I feel or behave.

These affirmations and their underlying meaning and message will empower you in realizing how to heal your inner child.

I hope these affirmations help you to connect with your inner child and find ways to heal emotionally from the past. When you use these affirmations on a regular basis, you will start to feel immense empathy for your inner child. The more involved you become in this process, the more rewarding it will be for you as a whole person.

Start a Healing Journal

In our quiet moments, we can connect with our inner child through writing. This helps us to express ourselves. There are various ways to begin this process, but I want to share a few of them with you:

A common method is by tracing your family tree and listing your personal experiences and emotions that come up as you do so. You can also write down various things that have been done to harm you as well as those things that have been done for you.

This exercise is helpful in strengthening your ability to reflect on the past and use that strength to heal yourself.

Another method is writing about a special theme you choose for each week. For instance, I have journaled about the following topics:

1. How I feel about my inner child:

The main reason I wrote about this was to remind myself that this was a relationship – and one that should be strengthened.

2. What my inner child feels like:

I wrote about how loving and nurturing my inner child is, and what they need from me to feel safe and secure.

3. Why I feel the way I do towards my inner child:

The main reason for this was to help me understand why I feel such a strong sense of empathy for them, especially since we've spent the better part of our lives emotionally estranged from one another.

4. My relationship with my inner child as a child. I described how it looked as well as what it sounded like as a child.

5. How I have acted towards my inner child as an adult:

This was meant to help me better take into account the fact that I have grown up and now have the ability to see the person that my inner child really is.

6. What has been done for me by my inner child?

This was about strengthening our relationship by letting them know how much good they have done for me, but also making sure they know what is expected of them as well as what is needed.

7. What has been done to me by my inner child?

This was done for the same reasons as above.

This exercise will teach you many things about your inner child, including how they may have acted in childhood and how they may be acting in the present day. You will use this information to continue on your journey of emotional healing.

Writing a Letter to Your Inner Child

Writing letters to your inner child can be effective for many reasons. It is empowering because you get the chance to express yourself freely. It helps foster a deeper bond between you and your inner child, which can lead to more loving relationships in other aspects of your life. It also helps you gain a new perspective on the things that have happened in your life. You get the chance to see things from another's perspective which helps you feel less over emotional about them.

Many things can be explored through the letter. Here are some questions you might want to ask yourself:

Do I feel safe telling my inner child the truth about what happened in my childhood? Why or why not?

Am I afraid of facing or dealing with what has gone on in my past? Explain.

If my inner child could speak with me today, what would he/she say? Would she tell me that I have made the right decisions in life or that I still have more healing to do?

How do I want to improve the relationship between my inner child and me? What can I do so it is easier for us to communicate with each other freely?

How would things be different if my childhood had been happy and harmonious?

What can I do so that her childhood will remain happy and harmonious in my mind?

What can I do so my adulthood will be happy and harmonious?

I hope these questions give you some ideas of what you can include in your letter to your inner child.

You may also want to include questions that are specific to the struggles you had when you were a kid or still have now that you're an adult. This helps you to become more aware of how your past issues might be affecting present day problems, which will make it easier for you to confront them.

Letters to your inner child can be written in your journal or in a letter format. This exercise will strengthen your ability to express yourself freely and honestly, without fear of hurting the feelings of others. It will also help you in becoming more aware of how your childhood may have influenced how you are living in the present.

Writing a Letter to Yourself from Your Inner Child

This exercise will help you become more aware of how your inner child might be affecting your present day life.

It is helpful to write out a plan for what you might want to happen in your future. This can help you determine if any changes are needed in the inner child's behavior. You may decide that you need to give it more boundaries or that it needs more nurturing. You can also decide that you need to give it more freedom, which will allow it to grow in confidence and independence.

We all want to feel secure and happy. We want to be able to trust the people around us so we can get the help we need when we need it. It is no different for inner children. This exercise will be very beneficial in helping your inner child really feel loved and valued for who they are. It will help them feel great about themselves, which is something that they may have never had.

This process can be done in many ways. You can write the letter to yourself when you were a child or when you are an adult. You can write it to your adult self for your inner child to read when they are grown up.

This exercise can help you become aware of your inner child's needs so that you can better meet them in the present day. This will benefit your relationships between these two parts of yourself.

It is important to remember that not every letter will reveal all the answers you are looking for. That is why it is important to do this exercise as many times as you feel necessary. Write the letter from your inner child to yourself as many times as you need.

The goal is to find ways to meet your inner child's needs in a present day way. It is important for it to know that its needs are important and that they still matter now and always will.

This is a unique exercise and can be done in any way that feels comfortable for you and your inner child.

CHAPTER 12: EMPLOY THE POWER OF VISUALIZATION FOR YOUR BENEFIT

When it comes to healing, visualization is a powerful tool. It can be used to heal mental, emotional, and physical problems. It accomplishes this by focusing your mind on the healing process. When you visualize, your mind sends signals that help you heal by performing certain functions or processes that are necessary for that process to occur.

This will help you strengthen your mental abilities, which can be applied to achieve other goals as well. Visualization has also been proven to help patients recover from traumas that happened many years ago. The process of visualization actually brings these memories to life within a person's mind. The memories become alive and present in the person's mind, which can then help to heal that particular issue or memory.

In some cases, visualization can have a direct effect on the body. Regarding these cases, it has been proven that simple things such as spending time walking in nature can be just as effective as taking more traditional medications. Studies show that the benefit of walking in nature is just as effective at reducing stress levels, improving well-being, and reducing life-threatening illnesses.

Visualization is a very powerful tool. You can use it to help you heal your inner child by asking them questions about their experiences or issues they may be having.

Visualization can also be used to help you create the life that you really want. Once you are able to see your life as you want it to be, you can then begin to visualize yourself living that life. As you do this, more of the things within that vision will start coming into your reality.

The great thing about visualization is that it can help you create the life that you want right now, as well as the life that you want to live in the future. You can also see past events and change them so they won't happen again. For example, if you had a bad relationship with your father in the past, you can use visualization to change that memory. You can then see yourself having a good relationship with him in the present or future.

Visualization is also a great tool for your inner child because it allows them to speak directly to you. It is essential for them to be able to do this so they can tell you what they are really feeling without any fear of rejection or abandonment.

You can also use visualization to help your inner child change things in their life. This can be done by visualizing them taking steps towards the life they really want. Visualize them taking these steps, accomplishing these goals or making these changes in their life.

When you begin visualizing, it may feel awkward or uncomfortable, especially if you are not used to it. Put your mind at ease by thinking of something that is very pleasant to you.

Look at this image for a few moments. Close your eyes and imagine this is happening right in front of you. Really see it in your mind. Imagine that you are really there, experiencing what you are seeing. Take note of how things look, feel, smell and taste in your mind's eye.

Visualize the things that are pleasing to you or bring about feelings of acceptance or love for yourself. You can also visualize yourself doing things that please or comfort you, such as receiving or giving love. Focus on the details of what you are seeing. If you see something moving, try to picture it moving in slow motion so you can really see every detail.

While the above exercise may seem very simple, it is actually very powerful. Visualizing something on an infinite level is one of the most advanced forms of visualization there is. It can help you to heal things in your mind.

After this exercise, take the time to sit and allow yourself to feel comfortable with what you have done. This is something that takes time to master, so don't expect it to be perfect right away. Continue practicing visualization, and you will see how well it can help you to heal your inner child.

Music Therapy for Healing Your Inner Child

One method that can help you heal your inner child is to use music as a healing tool. There are many different ways that music therapy can be used, including in meditation. Meditation can help you clear your mind, so you can feel much better and more positive about life in general. Music has a powerful effect on your emotions, so it can help you feel much more relaxed and calm.

A lot of people think that music is just for listening or dancing to, but it can help you heal many issues in your life. Music is very effective at helping you to move past difficult experiences in your life without feeling too much pain.

Music can help your inner child release negative emotions. It can also help them to feel more positive about themselves and about their lives so they have higher self-esteem. This is very powerful because it makes your inner child feel more accepted and loved by you.

Another benefit to music therapy is that it can help you recognize what emotions you are experiencing in the present moment. This may seem strange since music isn't directly causing these feelings, but it can be very effective nonetheless. By feeling your emotions when you listen to music, you will learn how to recognize what they are in situations where they are not so obvious.

There are many different types of music that you can use to help your inner child heal. This can include rock, classical, gospel, folk or anything else that you like. However, keep in mind that particular types of music will work better for different situations than others.

If your inner child is extremely angry at you because of things that happened in the past, it may be beneficial to use slow reggae or rock music. Music can be very versatile and it works in many different ways, depending on the situation.

You should also consider what kind of music you normally listen to or use to relax. It may be helpful to work with this kind of music in order to feel more comfortable in allowing yourself to heal your inner child.

If you're having trouble with your inner child's behavior, because of past traumatic events, it may be preferable to use soothing music. This can include music that has a lot of string sounds. The ideal type of music should include a lot of high-frequency sounds and easily distinguishable melodies.

Be aware that the healing process is not one that just happens overnight. You can rely on music therapy to help your inner child for many years to come.

Emotions are very powerful, and they can easily overtake your conscious thoughts if you let them. When you feel negative emotions towards your past self, take a moment to slow down and look at what's going on inside you and your inner child. This will help you to regain control, and it will make it easier for you to feel more positive about your life.

You may also experience some of the same emotions that your inner child is feeling, which can make things even more complicated. This is why it is very necessary that you focus on healing your inner child as much as possible. It will help you control your emotions and feel better about life in general.

Be sure to stay as positive as possible as you work through this. This can help you avoid feeling overwhelmed by your emotions and it will smooth out some of the rough spots in the healing process. One strategy that can be helpful is to make a note of every time you feel an emotion and try not to allow yourself to dwell on these negative memories or thoughts for very long.

You may also want to try and explore some of the emotions your inner child is feeling. They may very well be hiding some negative emotions towards you, but it is important that you try to find out what they are and how you can help them heal.

There are various ways that you can use music as a healing tool, and everybody will have different results. There is no such thing as the right or wrong way to use music; it will depend on your life experience. However, using music as a healing tool is very powerful, and you will see how it can benefit your life after many years of use.

CHAPTER 13: EMPLOY THE POWER OF MEDITATION FOR YOUR BENEFIT

Meditation is something that I find very healing. It can be a great way to release pent-up emotions and to reduce the stress and anxiety that we all experience at different points in our lives. There are different kinds of meditation, and some of them are specifically geared towards helping you to heal your inner child.

When you meditate, you should try to focus on one thing only. This will help you to calm your mind so that you can feel much more centered and content within yourself. This is not an easy task, but it can be very powerful if you are able to achieve it.

People who meditate regularly often have a much easier time with healing their inner child because they are better at controlling their emotions. When your mind is racing, you will have a harder time moving past your emotions and healing your inner child. By learning how to meditate, you will reduce these distractions so that you can heal yourself without too much difficulty.

You can meditate by focusing on breathing. Breathing is something that everybody does every day. You do not even need to be consciously thinking about it, but if you are breathing correctly, you will be releasing toxins from your body through the process.

You will find many different benefits to meditation when it comes to your life in general. You will be able to feel more like yourself and less like an impostor. You will also be better at controlling your emotions and you will be better able to deal with the situations that come up each day.

When you are ready to start meditating, I recommend that you make it a daily habit. At first, you should try to do it for about 15 minutes every day. If 15 minutes doesn't seem like enough time to give your mind a chance to calm down, then try doing it for 30 minutes instead.

The more you meditate, the easier it will be for you to relax and reduce negative emotions that are causing problems in your life. Watch out for any negative emotions that might arise during your meditation because it can easily overwhelm you and ruin what you are trying to accomplish.

This is a very powerful way to heal yourself, and it can help you to feel much better about who you are as a person. You will learn how to deal with this difficult period of your life by working through the lessons that your inner child can teach you.

Be Patient with Yourself

It is necessary that you remain patient with yourself, no matter what is going on in your life. At the beginning of this process, you may not feel like you are making much progress, but that does not mean that your emotions are not healing. It just means that there is still healing that needs to take place. You will begin to notice positive changes after several months of emotional release, but the process can take time.

It can be very frustrating to try and work through a difficult issue because you may feel as though you are not making any progress. You may become frustrated with yourself because you do not think that your situation is getting any better. At that point, it is important for you to step away from trying to solve your problem and allow yourself to heal at a much deeper level.

You may feel like you need to get back into your problem in order for this process to work, but this is not true at all. You need to give your mind a chance to heal on a deeper level. When this happens, you will be able to notice the changes that are taking place in your life because your emotions will be less intense.

One thing you should always keep in mind is that other people's opinions do not matter when it comes to healing from trauma. For example, you may have been told by somebody that meditation does not work, but just because it didn't work for them doesn't mean it won't work for you.

It is not always easy to step away from trying to solve your problem during the process of inner child healing, but this is an essential part of the process. If you are able to remain patient with yourself during this time, you will notice much more positive change in your life after several months have passed.

This is the only way to heal yourself at the deepest level. If you take things too quickly, you will find that your issues are getting worse and that your inner child is suffering even more than before.

If you do not see any positive changes in your life after several months, take a step back and look at ways to move forward. At this point, you may need to look at different forms of healing. This is not the time to give up on the process, but it is time to make adjustments.

As you continue to work on your healing , it is important to pay close attention to your emotions. Your emotions can change very quickly, and they may cause you to get frustrated with the process of inner child healing. You will lose more of yourself if you get fed up with the process and then start trying to solve your problems too quickly. This is why it is so important for you to take things very slowly during the healing process.

Channeling Your Inner Child

Whenever you try to work through your issues as an adult, you may struggle to deal with the things that are affecting you. You may feel very confused and unaware of what you need in order to feel better. If your feelings conflict with your actions, it will be difficult for you to get what you need out of life.

You can heal yourself by channeling your inner child. This is one of the best ways to heal at the deepest level, but it is important to make sure you are doing this correctly. You need to make sure that you are dealing with the right emotions, and this can be difficult for some people.

You may not always be able to tell what emotions you are experiencing during the process of inner child healing. This is where many people get so confused. You need to be able to look at yourself and recognize what emotions you are experiencing.

If you are not able to do so, it may be because your inner child has trapped you in fantasy. You may find it beneficial to work with other people who understand the process of channeling and healing the inner child. It is very important to take advantage of all of the resources that are available to you.

If you are working with a therapist or a support group, you will be able to get the help that you need. This is where it can be very important for you to communicate your feelings with others. You will need the guidance of someone who knows how to help you during this process, but it can help others work through their issues as well. If you cannot afford to work with a therapist, take the time to read books and listen to audio recordings.

Take action even when you do not feel motivated to do so. When you can see your emotions more clearly, it will be easier for you to make progress on your healing journey. You will be able to recognize what you need in order to feel better, and you may not need the support of other people as much.

The sooner that you take action, the better. You will need to be ready for this because it may require you to make substantial changes in your life. If you do not want to go back to the way you were before, you will need to be willing to accept these changes.

CHAPTER 14: ATTAINING INNER STRENGTH FOR THE RESTORATION OF ONE'S INNER CHILD

You have learned to take care of yourself. You know that the only way to live a happy and fulfilling life is by caring for your emotional, mental, and physical wellbeing. You know that you can create in your life what you feel in your heart and that you must parent yourself in the same way that you parent your children. There are lots of ways to accomplish personal growth and healing through inner child work. But the most important thing is to take action!

One great way to empower your inner child is by becoming an active member of an online community. These communities are filled with positive, supportive people who will welcome you with open arms, wherever you are on your healing journey. You'll have opportunities to share your triumphs and your struggles with people who understand what you're going through. Everyone in the community will really want you to succeed. They will want to cheer for you and give you a virtual hug when times are difficult. And even though they aren't physically there, these people will be a part of your healing process.

A significant part of inner child work is learning how to forgive yourself and accept yourself unconditionally, flaws and all. That's why it's so beneficial to be a part of an online community of supportive people. Nobody is perfect, but the members of the community are there to love you just as you are. They can empathize with your imperfections, knowing that they have their own strengths and weaknesses. And they can encourage you to forgive yourself for your mistakes, knowing that they've made some pretty big blunders themselves!

Another way to achieve empowerment is to write in a journal, on a blog, do artwork, or expressing your thoughts and emotions in another creative way. Journaling is a great way to gain insight into yourself. It's also a great way to release emotions that you might be suppressing. In writing about them with the intention of freeing yourself from them with acceptance and love, you can make true progress on the path toward inner healing.

Writing about your feelings can have a positive influence on your physical well-being. Studies prove that writing down your thoughts and feelings reduces stress hormones, increases immune system activity, and greatly improves the functioning of the heart muscle. When you feel emotionally overwhelmed or physically ill, try journaling about it in an effort to decrease negative emotions and increase emotional wellness.

Another way to gain empowerment for your inner child is through the creative arts. Many people have found that creative expression helps them to express themselves and heal from their inner pain. There are a number of different creative arts that you can explore for yourself, but painting, writing, photography, singing, or performing anxiety-reducing music is one of the best ways to release your emotions and heal from the pain of your inner child.

If you're a musician, consider writing music as an empowerment exercise for your inner child. Remember, it's not about your skill as a musician; it's about the emotional strength you gain from expressing yourself, and releasing your emotions in a way that is healing to yourself. Explore the music you make and give yourself permission to share it with others.

The other way you can nurture yourself is through spiritual growth. One of the brilliant ways to explore your spirituality is through religious study. You may not be content with the religion in which you were raised. You may even be searching for a new religion to call your own. Whatever your situation, it's important that you seek spiritual fulfillment in some capacity. Otherwise, you'll never feel like you're totally connected to everything around you.

You may not know it, but you're on the road to inner child healing every time you nurture yourself in any of these ways. When you feel empowered in your life, you'll be much better equipped to make positive changes in the world around you. The people in your life will benefit from your presence in a multitude of ways. But the most important person in your life is YOU. Always remember that you are the driving force behind your success! You deserve to bask in the glow of your own empowerment.

Inner Child Development

The more you learn regarding yourself, the more you'll understand how unique you are. As times change, your identity is continually being shaped into a unique individual. After all, you are one person with many purposes. You have desires that need to be expressed and experiences that need to be learned. Your inner child makes sure that these things get accomplished in the most efficient manner possible, whether it's through positive or negative actions.

Honoring your inner child is all about understanding yourself. The better you understand your emotions, the more effective you'll be in building a life that is truly satisfying. You might not always get it right the very first time, but you'll get it right eventually because every decision you make in life is an opportunity to enrich yourself in some way.

The more you learn about yourself, the more you'll understand what your needs are. As a child, you were likely not allowed to express your needs and desires. You may have been frequently ignored and disappointed by the adults in your life, which left you feeling incredibly confused and scared. You couldn't understand why you weren't being taken care of and how things could be better. But now you can. You can take back the control that was taken from you as a child by expressing your needs and desires so that they can be met.

Please don't think that you're "too old" to express yourself. Remember, it is never too late to start over and try something new. You can learn so much about yourself by trying something new. You may find that the past doesn't define you, after all...

The more you learn about yourself, the more you'll be able to understand how your emotions are affecting your life. You may have been taught that it was your job to suppress your feelings in order for everyone else to be happy. But it's the right time to let go of that mindset. You need to know how your emotions are affecting you internally if you want to be empowered. It's time to let your emotions run free.

You may have even been taught that it was your job to suppress your emotions in order to not get into trouble. But it's time to step into the world and see how you're performing in the face of every challenge that may come your way. You don't need anyone else to tell you what kind of person you are – there is much more depth in how proud of yourself you'll feel when you allow yourself to act on any negative feelings that arise.

The more you learn about yourself, the more you'll be able to understand the emotions that you're feeling in any given situation. You'll be able to identify emotions that have been causing you pain in the past and work through them so that they no longer influence your life negatively. You'll be able to accept feelings that have been plaguing you because of a previous experience. And eventually, these emotions will disappear from your life because you refuse to let them continue to have an effect on your life.

As you keep on learning more about yourself and your inner child, you'll be able to identify and release any detrimental emotions that have been causing you pain. And when that happens, your life will be changed forever. You will have taken control of your mind – your thoughts and feelings – and will no longer be a slave to them. Instead, you'll be the master of your own destiny.

You're beyond the need for anyone else to tell you how to live or feel. You're not a child anymore. And you're no longer a slave to the things that have happened to you in your past. You're a self-aware adult who is now in control of your life. Your emotional wounds have been dealt with and hopefully healed, so that they can no longer affect you or those around you adversely.

It's never too late to learn how to make decisions that are best for you. It's time to stand up and take control of your life.

Ease Your Childhood Pain

As an adult, you can learn to work through some of the pain that you've been experiencing since you were a child. You can learn new ways to handle old problems and make new decisions about how you want your life to be. But first, you'll need to do some self-healing. That's where your inner child comes in...

Your inner child is a piece of your mind that remembers how it felt when you were a child.

You're a strong and powerful adult now, but sometimes even adults aren't aware of how much pain their childhood has inflicted on them. You may have been raised in a way that is actively hurting you now. Or you may have been conditioned to want things that aren't good for you. You may be carrying around a lot of self-loathing and doubt because of the things that happened to you in the past. It's okay to feel pain about these things. That doesn't make you weak, it makes you human. It's the way your inner child was taught to respond when dealing with deep pain.

There's nothing wrong with feeling pain. It's okay to go numb in certain situations, even when it comes to trying new things within yourself. You are allowed to feel the kind of pain you feel, so long as you are able to let it go without affecting the people around you.

So many adults don't allow themselves to express their feelings because they're worried that it will be detrimental to them. But often, these adults are simply allowing their inner child to stop them from reaching their full potential. If you want your life to be happy and fulfilling, you need to heal any wounds that your inner child is holding onto.

These are some ways to help you ease your pain from childhood:

Write about how you feel.

Writing is a great way to start working through your pain because it allows you to convey your thoughts and emotions in a safe space. It's important for you to remember that all of the negative emotions that you're feeling are not necessarily bad for you, even though they may feel like it at first. There are good things to be gained from them, even though it may not seem that way. You can start letting go of these old wounds by expressing your emotions through your writing or journaling.

Make a list of what you're feeling.

Create a journal or an email list of things that you're feeling. Putting them down on paper can help you recognize and acknowledge your uncomfortable feelings.

Do things that remind you of the emotions.

You can ease your pain from childhood by remembering some of the emotions your actions gave rise to. You can do this by doing the following:

- Putting on certain music

- Listening to an old song or album

- Watching a movie

- Reading a book or article that made you feel something in the past

- Going to the location where the memory occurred

Meditate on how you felt in different situations.

It can be extremely helpful for your inner child to meditate on some of the problems that they've encountered in their life. This practice will help you work through the emotions and come out on the other side in a better place. It also helps you gain a better understanding of how you felt in different situations.

Get rid of any negative feelings.

It's a good idea to get rid of any old feelings that you've been holding onto for too long. You may do this by doing the following:

- Cutting up photos that you no longer need.

- Tearing up cards and letters that hold negative emotions for you.

- Burning the things that remind you of difficult times.

Make some changes in your life.

Over time, these changes will make you feel better about yourself. You'll start to let go of some of the old feelings that your inner child is still holding onto. You'll start to free up some space in your mind for new and better ideas. You will learn how to take control of your pain from childhood and become a stronger, more capable person. But you can't do this unless you make changes in your life...

Take the time to create a list of goals that you've been meaning to work on for a while now. These goals could be anything from getting fit to improving your relationships with family members. You can break these goals down into sections that you need to work on.

Reach out to people who could help you.

You might not be able to do it alone, so reach out to people who care about you and would like to see you become a better person. You can go back to those relationships from your childhood and ask them for help in the same way that they tried helping you when you were a kid.

Speak up for yourself if people are hurting your feelings.

If a friend or a loved one is hurting your feelings, up yourself. Say something like, "That makes me feel uncomfortable." This will give them the chance to stop their behavior and apologize.

Learn to push through the pain

Pain can be used as a way of motivating yourself in order to reach goals and accomplish things in your life. This is not easy, but it does help you to achieve everything that you want for yourself.

While there are many things that are out of your control, you can still use your pain from childhood as a way of becoming a better person. You might have suffered abuse or the trauma during your childhood, but this doesn't mean that you don't have positive memories in there somewhere...hidden between all the bad ones.

So work through the pain – even if it doesn't make sense to you. Use it as a way to become a better person.

You can't do this whole "healing" process overnight. You need to work at it over time, but that doesn't mean that you won't see any results while you're doing it. So work on yourself slowly and steadily. Remember that betterment does not come by accident – it has to be intentional and something that you do over time.

Treat this as a productive activity that will benefit you in the long run. Trust your instincts and stop blaming yourself for feeling these negative emotions. You can be better than this. You can be so much more than the little boy or girl who's been hurt over and over again. You can take control of your life and you can do so without being so afraid of your own pain.

Release Your Childhood Guilt

A very challenging thing for many people to do is to let go of the guilt that they feel for actions that they committed as a child. Your parents may even have actually drilled this guilt into you when you were growing up.

It might seem like whatever it is that you did, it's unforgivable. And this kind of persistent guilt could be affecting all aspects of your life. Children don't have a fully developed conscience, so guilt can become a driving force.

But the negative feelings you experience because of your childhood are not your fault. You did not deserve whatever happened to you. These feelings are based on things that have become distorted in your mind due to the way you've been raised.

Guilt can become an inner child's worst nightmare It's tempting to continue to feel guilty about what happened in the past, whether it actually happened or not. But you have to remember that guilt is just an emotion that comes up in your mind. This has nothing to do with the reality of the situation.

To release your childhood guilt you should practice letting go of the guilt that comes up inside of you every time something happens in the present day. When you can learn to let go of guilt, it won't become an emotional burden for your inner child. This new way of viewing the reality of your past will stop you feeling so hurt, and you'll be able to get on with the business of your adult life.

One important thing you can do to release your childhood guilt is to look for any good things that happened as a result of the situation. Maybe there were family members who died, but maybe you also had a chance to save someone from a situation that was going to cause serious pain. How can you look at the situation from a different perspective? You have been learning life lessons from this bad situation in your past. So look for the good things about the event and let go of any guilt that comes up in your mind when you're thinking about it. It's not easy to do this, but it will help your inner child get rid of the guilt that is hurting him or her.

It's also very important to focus on ending the guilt that comes up in your mind when you are under stress. For example, you may feel a lot of guilt if you have a bad day at work and don't get anything accomplished. It feels good to close up shop and go home, but you can still have a lot of residual feelings about how you messed up that day. So when you get home after work, tell yourself that you did the best you could under the circumstances. Tell yourself that you'd like to think about the events of the day more later on, but for now, it's time to relax and put things in perspective.

It's also a great idea to make a list of all the things in your life that make you feel guilty. This might seem like a strange thing to do, but it will help make your inner child feel safer and more secure. When you have a list of things you feel guilty about, you may come to see that nothing horrible actually happened as a result of these things. In fact, you didn't have any control over that person or their actions at all.

You can also make a list of all the things you did when you were growing up that made your parents happy. This is very important because it will help you to start seeing your childhood in a new light.

You can also learn how to forgive yourself for making mistakes as an adult. If you feel guilty about something you did in the past, it's very common to make yourself feel guilty for years after. Even if there is nothing you can do to change the past, it's important to surrender these feelings of guilt. Remind yourself that there are thousands of people who have done worse things than you did – and many of them probably haven't learned how to forgive themselves yet. It's also important to remember that the past is just that – the past. It will never be repeated, so it's time for you to let go of any guilt that you might still be feeling.

If you find that these tips aren't working for you, it might be time to see a counselor. Guilt can become an emotional burden for your inner child if it's allowed to continue unchecked. The good news is there are trained counselors who can help you get rid of years of guilt in a short amount of time. Best of all, a counselor can give you a new perspective on past events so you can start seeing things differently.

Guilt is a very strong emotion, but it doesn't have to poison your life. Having an understanding of how your inner child feels might help you forgive yourself, and it can also help you release the guilt that has been sitting inside your mind for years.

Once you learn how to release your childhood guilt, it is a good idea to go back and examine moments from your past. There's a chance that you have been carrying around some guilt for something that happened long ago, and you didn't even know it. But once you understand how your inner child feels, it will be easier for you to forgive yourself.

Accessing Blocked Memories

As you grow older, the events of your past will become less vivid in your mind. And there's no telling what memories you might have that are blocked from your consciousness. You might have blocks in your mind that are keeping you from accessing memories that are important to you today.

These blocks could be keeping important memories out of your consciousness because they're connected to something in the present day. For example, if you feel really bad about something someone did to you in the past, it can be hard to let go of those feelings because they're tied up with the present action. The more you think about why you are holding these feelings inside of you, the more important it becomes for you to let them go.

There's no telling what kind of stress or anxiety might be causing these blocks. Even if you are unable to remember these events from the past, they could be affecting you in ways you don't even realize. And it's possible that these memories are really important for you to have at this time in your life. So it's crucial for you to learn how to access these memories.

To get your mind to let go of the memories it's block out, you need to learn how to access your subconscious. If you can learn how to do so, you can get rid of blocks that are keeping certain memories out of your consciousness. You can access the subconscious behind you by using your imagination. Just imagine that your consciousness is behind your eyes. And then imagine that the part of your mind that is blocking out these memories can be removed by feeling it flow down into your body. Then imagine that the memories are coming back into your consciousness, and you will soon start to remember the events of the past.

You might feel a lot of anxiety or even lightheadedness when you first start to remember some of these memories. It's because all of this information is coming into your mind at one time. Use these feelings as an indicator that your mind is starting to release the blocks that are keeping these memories away from you.

Use your imagination to go back into your childhood and remember the details from when you were a child. Focus on the things you remember about yourself as a child. The more your mind is connected with the consciousness that is behind you, the closer it will be connected with the memories that have been blocked from being remembered.

It might also help to talk with someone about your past. When you're having a hard time remembering some memories, talk to this person and ask them to give you a description of the event as they remember it. You might also want to tell this person why it's so important for you to remember these events – especially if they're really painful. Then the person can help you to break down the barrier in your mind that is preventing you from accessing these memories.

If you're having a hard time accessing the memories on your own, then it might be a good idea to seek professional help.

Many of us have painful memories that we would like to release, but we are unable to access them in order to do so. It's because of our guilt and shame that we keep these memories blocked out of our consciousness. Give yourself permission to remember the events of your childhood, and try to access your subconsciousness. If you can do this, then you will be able to break down the barriers that are keeping your memory away.

Think of these memories as being like two sections of your mind. The first section is the part of your mind that's responsible for what goes on around you. And the other part is the consciousness behind you – the subconscious. Often, these parts don't get along with each other, which is why you keep blocks in your mind that keep some things away from you.

If you remember something about yourself that's embarrassing or painful, then try to stop blaming yourself for it. Tell yourself it's OK to make mistakes. Just forgive yourself for whatever happened, and play back the scene from your memory in your mind. Then see if you can get the part of your mind that is blocking this scene away from you. If you can get rid of these barriers in your mind, then the images of these scenes will pop into your consciousness with ease.

See these scenes as playing out before your eyes like a movie. You can do this with whatever memory you'd like to remember, and whatever event or experience you'd like to understand better.

It can be hard to get rid of all the emotions attached to these memories. But if you do anything that will get you back in touch with your true feelings, then your mind will start releasing these emotions and you can become a healthier person in this life.

Accessing your subconscious will help you to unlock the secrets of your past. The more you try to remember these events, the better off you'll be.

Healing Through Deep Breathing Exercises

Deep breathing is another way to connect and heal your inner child. It connects us with our emotional selves, which we often neglect in an attempt to escape from emotional pain. It can be such a relief to finally begin to connect with that part of ourselves. It is like the difference between living inside a dark, cramped room and suddenly being able to open up all the window shades and let in the light, fresh air and visibility.

When you are confidently breathing deeper into your body, letting more of your emotional energy move through you more easily, you are in the right space for some emotional exercises. What follows are several exercises that will help you connect with your inner child.

Connecting with your inner child through your breathing

The first step is to become comfortable with deep breathing. It's okay if you feel silly at first. This is not something you should be doing for show or for others. We are working with the real part of ourselves...our inner child. There is an innocence, a child-like quality to this exercie...which means there's nothing to get "right" or "wrong", "better" or "worse." Begin by noticing your breath. Notice how you breathe right now, the natural rhythm of your breathing. Then notice how it changes when you in-tentionally breathe more deeply into your body. Each time you inhale, try to draw in more air into the lower part of your lungs. Hold it for a few seconds and then exhale, letting the air flow out from the bottom of your lungs. You will naturally find that you breathe more deeply if you imagine yourself breathing into a place in your body where there is a lot of tension or pain. Try to slow down the rate at which you are breathing, but don't force it. Breathing more deeply will begin to relax you and put you into a meditative state. It may feel awkward at first, but just relax...and breathe...

Exercises

1. Think of those times when you were angry or upset with someone, perhaps because they did something unkind, disrespectful or hurtful. Try to recall how you felt and what you did next. Perhaps something that happened later made you feel better. How did the anger affect your life?

2. Make peace with someone else who has upset you in the past, perhaps by validating their behavior...or maybe by forgiving them. Then notice how it affects your life now.

3. Think of a time when you were upset with yourself. Try to recall how you felt then and what you did next. Perhaps something that happened later made you feel better. How did the "self-anger" affect your life?

4. Make peace with yourself, perhaps by forgiving your past mistakes...even if they were serious... Then notice how it affects your life now.

5. Think of something that you feel terrible about now or that you regret doing. Try to recall how you felt then and what you

did next. Perhaps something later made you feel better, but only because it validated the pain or made it go away...but also because it made you feel worse to be reminded of what hap pened...perhaps because nothing could ever make up for what happened. What about the ones you made cry, the ones you hurt...how did you feel when they cried? How did that make you feel?

6. Imagine someone in your life who has hurt you deeply in some form or other...maybe it was a friend, perhaps a lover ...maybe your brother or sister, maybe it was your parent or child...maybe someone who was supposed to be protecting you. See them standing in front of you and look into their eyes. Lift your hand toward them gently and extend it out toward them as though you were going to touch them...but don't touch them...not yet. Take a breath and hold it just for a moment. ..look at the pain in their eyes...and imagine you can see your pain reflected back. Are you ready to forgive them? Or does that make it too real? Maybe you feel that they should have known better, that they did it on purpose, or that they've been given a chance before and they've blown it...what if this time they won't blow it? What if this time, for some reason...you trust them...completely...would you extend your hand to touch theirs? Could you forgive them? Or not?

It may take a little time to forgive others and it may take a little longer to forgive yourself.

Remember, you can do it...and you have to, if you want your life back...

CHAPTER 15: WHAT MAKES INNER CHILD RECOVERY CRUCIAL?

Many of us are stuck consciously thinking about ourselves only as adults, but our dreams are trying to tell us something different. Not just our dreams, but how we feel in general. That's why it's important for us to remember that the inner child is still there and cannot be suppressed or ignored. That energy will continue to work its way into your daily life until you release it. And when you do release it, you will feel lighter.

Darkness cannot be suppressed. It has to be felt and accepted in order to move on, just like anger or sadness or frustration or joy or pain. We all have our own unique layers of darkness that we have accumulated over the years and it's not our fault – it's just a process of being human. There is no one who can avoid it completely.

You cannot be happy if you are in conflict with yourself. How do you think it's possible to be in conflict with yourself? It's possible if you deny an aspect of yourself, an integral part of your being that makes up who you are. That would be the inner child. If you deny the inner child's existence, then there is an aspect of yourself that will continue to cause problems as it works its way out into your daily life.

If you're having problems in your relationships, there's a good chance you are rejecting part of yourself. The more you are willing to look at the ways in which you are failing yourself, the better off you will be. You can't truly love other people if you don't love yourself. You can't accept other people if you reject yourself.

When we deny particular aspects of our personality, it can cause us to feel stuck. We can feel like something is wrong with us, but it isn't. It's just that we are trying to love ourselves in a way that doesn't feel right because we're still locked into an outdated belief system of what's acceptable and unacceptable to ourselves. So if you can begin to see how much you've denied yourself, you'll begin to understand why everything appears to be going wrong for no reason at all.

When people think of healing their inner child, they think of childhood issues. That's not what this is about. Inner child healing is about finding your real feelings. The feelings that were lost when you learned how to "fit in," to survive in the world by conforming to what society told you was acceptable. In other words, it's about bringing out the truth of who you are.

Why is inner child healing important? Because when an aspect of yourself continues to come up in your life as a problem, that aspect needs attention. It needs acknowledgment. It needs to be accepted. It needs to be allowed to do its work so you can clear it out of your system.

Our inner child is the part of ourselves that we carry around in our hearts, memories, and thoughts. It represents everything that we wish to protect or ignore because it feels painful. With this in mind, it's easy to see why healing your inner child can be helpful for both mental and physical wellbeing.

There are many ways of handling stress, some better than others. Many individuals turn to alcohol or other addictive substances when trying to cope with stress. However, while this may make you feel better in the short term, it creates additional problems in the long term.

If alcohol or drugs are used too often, they can cause health problems and addiction issues that affect every aspect of your life. These include family relationships, financial issues, employment difficulties, and legal problems. Addiction can also cause serious health issues including liver damage and high blood pressure.

Inner child healing is a way of dealing with stress without turning to alcohol or other substances. It is a technique that focuses on learning how to listen and comfort your inner child. The more you learn to do this, the less you will need substances as a coping mechanism for stress. You can learn how to take deep, slow breaths and truly listen to your feelings and memories without judgment. This may be difficult initially, but as you practice it more often, it becomes easier.

Psychiatrists have also recognized the important role of inner child healing in treating patients struggling with severe disorders such as bipolar disorder, depression, anxiety disorders, and post-traumatic stress disorder. By helping patients learn how to soothe their emotions while understanding the roots of their internal struggles, psychiatrists are able to help them better manage their symptoms.

Inner child healing can help with both mental and physical well-being. When we heal the inner child, we learn to comfort our emotions and bring peace of mind. This can be used to combat stressful situations such as depression, anxiety, and even substance abuse. Inner child healing can lead to more confidence, happiness, and overall health.

The benefits of inner child healing can be found when we become aware of how much we deny ourselves. When we look into the face of our denial, we begin to understand why certain parts of ourselves continue to cause issues in our lives. It's because we've always denied that part of ourselves.

By becoming aware of our denial, we learn how to listen to who we are without judgment. When this occurs, we can begin to understand how much our stress levels put us in a state of denial. Denial is the process of ignoring the truth. It's where you refuse to acknowledge certain facts or feelings about yourself or others because the truth is too painful.

The more we deny the truth, the weaker our self-esteem becomes. This is because we're not accepting ourselves as individuals. Instead, we're always trying to be someone else in order to please those around us. When this occurs, it's because our inner child feels threatened. It feels as though its very existence will be challenged if it dares to be who it really is. That's the importance of inner child healing – to learn how to be real with yourself so you can bring your true self forward. This does not mean you have to change who you are or who you want to be. Inner child healing is about accepting the person you truly are in a way that feels safe, comfortable, and loving. By doing this, you can begin to release the pain associated with being in denial and with being someone else just to please others.

It's imperative for anyone who is interested in inner child healing to remember that it's a process. When we heal our inner child, we begin to feel the feelings that we've shut out for so long. It's important to stay positive and patient with yourself.

It can be tempting to want to rush through the process of healing your inner child because you don't like what you're feeling. However, you need to allow yourself time and space so you can learn the tools necessary for moving forward. The more you learn to soothe your inner child, the less you will need to rely on substances or other destructive coping mechanisms.

Tool and Resources

The following resources can help you to learn how to soothe your inner child, and accept yourself for who you are:

CBT

It's a great idea to read up on cognitive behavioral therapy, so you can learn how to change your thoughts and thinking patterns in a positive way. This is a form of meditation, and learning how to slow your thoughts is an important part of working with your inner child.

Breathing Exercises

If you've never done this before, it's important to take the time to learn how to breathe from your diaphragm. Many people breathe from their chest, but this is a shallow breath that may not help you soothe your inner child. When you breathe from your diaphragm, focus on the breath entering and exiting your body.

Therapy

Being able to talk out loud with a therapist will help you to better understand what it is you're feeling. If you don't have access to a therapist, journaling can also be useful for healing your inner child.

Positive Affirmations

Affirmations are a very powerful tool for healing and discovering who you really are. Use affirmations, such as "I am calm and relaxed" to help your inner child calm down and feel safe.

Control vs. Controlled Theory

The Control/Controlled Theory refers to the difference between being in control versus being controlled. When you are in control, you feel as though you have the power to change how your inner child feels. It will allow you to focus more on your positive outcomes. However, being controlled means that your inner child doesn't feel safe enough to trust, which can lead to feelings of depression, anxiety, and even substance abuse.

When it comes to healing your inner child, it's important to remember that you are doing it for yourself – not for others. The more you focus on yourself and understand how much you've been pushing down your emotions and feelings, the easier it becomes to accept who you truly are. When you can accept yourself, you can start to heal your inner child so you are able to recognize the difference between being in control and being controlled. This gives your inner child everything it needs to feel safe with itself so it can truly be happy with who it is. It's about remembering that "child" is a state of mind, not an age. It's about remembering how to be true to yourself so you can bring out the best in who you are. This is not be an easy task if you've always focused on protecting your inner child, but it's worth learning how to care for yourself again.

Understanding Your Inner Child

The way to help your inner child is to learn more about it. The better you understand why it's acting this way, the easier it will be for you to heal it and make a positive difference in your life.

Your inner child is the part of you that wants to be protected and nurtured. Your inner child wants to feel safe and secure, and it wants to be given the love it missed out on when you were growing up. Your inner child also needs attention in order to be happy. This could mean sharing your adult life with someone who loves you or getting the attention of others in some other way.

Your inner child may also be needy and demanding because it's never learned how to take care of itself. It's okay to get the things you need in life, but it's important to learn self-discipline and self-control, otherwise, you'll always be a burden on others. You want to feel loved and cared for, but you don't want to become a burden on the people in your life.

While you're working on healing your inner child, it's possible that you will struggle with low self-esteem and negative feelings about yourself. You were probably made to feel like you weren't good enough as a child, so now as an adult, you reject yourself as well.

The inner child knows how to enjoy life, but it doesn't know how to take care of itself. It wasn't taught these things when you were growing up. As soon as you learn these important lessons, your internal world will be transformed.

Your inner child can also be very angry and aggressive. If this is the case, chances are good that you have a lot of repressed thoughts regarding what happened in your past. These beliefs may have been traumatizing to your inner child, and it may be a very frightened and angry person. When a child is badly treated in his or her life, it's difficult for this individual to know how to behave properly as an adult.

Your inner child might also be sarcastic and difficult to deal with. It will find any reason it can to feel ashamed or lonely by pointing out the flaws in you as an adult. Your inner child may also be an expert at finding fault with others so that it can feel better about itself.

Your inner child may have unreal expectations of you – or no expectations at all. Sometimes this aspect of your personality will hold you to very strict standards, while other times it will let you do whatever you want without any consequences. A good relationship with your inner child depends on your ability to love yourself and accept who you are.

Your inner child will need a lot of support to cope with its anxieties and fears. It may also need professional help from a therapist. This can help you to learn to take control of your anxieties and heal the emotional wounds from the past. Over time, your inner child will learn how to love you for who you are as an adult. Many people don't really know how to love themselves as adults, so they have a hard time loving their inner child. Only by accepting the good and the bad in yourself will your inner child realize that it deserves love from those that it loves.

You can't change your inner child into someone that you want it to be. You can only heal them by learning to love yourself, even when you're falling short of your own expectations. This means you have to learn to give yourself time and space to be imperfect. It's normal to make mistakes, but you might be beating yourself up when you're feeling frustrated and angry. Learning how to forgive yourself will help your inner child feel safe and secure, and it'll help you to learn how to love yourself as well.

CHAPTER 16: CHALLENGES FACED WHEN REESTABLISHING A CONNECTION WITH YOUR INNER CHILD

If you have been struggling to reconnect with your inner child, then you have probably been experiencing some sort of obstacle that is preventing you from doing so. Below are some of the most common obstacles that prevent people from reconnecting with their inner child:

The biggest obstacle that prevents people from reconnecting with their inner child is fear. Many people are afraid of thinking about what they are missing out on by not being able to connect with their inner child.

This fear results in them making excuses. They always tell themselves that they have no time to reconnect with their inner child, or they have too many things to take care of.

The truth is that you can connect with your inner child whenever you want to. It does not need to be very time consuming. In fact, some people prefer to do it at little as five minutes a day.

So if fear is preventing you from reconnecting with your inner child, take some time to understand what exactly is holding you back. Once you have identified it, then find ways to start dealing with it. You can even try writing about how your fear makes you feel so that you are aware of all the reasons why it's holding you back.

Another obstacle that prevents many people from reconnecting with their inner child is a lack of energy. Most people have a hectic schedule where they work all day and then come home in the evening to take care of their family. By the time you finally get some free time, you feel like you don't have any energy left in your body.

To reconnect with your inner child, you need to find some time when you can be relaxed and happy. That is the only way that you can look inside your mind and find your inner child. If time feels like something you simply do not have, you might need to make some sacrifices in order to reconnect with yourself.

It's important to realize that reconnecting with your inner child can be extremely beneficial. It will help you live a happier life and feel more relaxed about everything around you. But if you are so busy with work, family, and other responsibilities that you have no time to do anything else, then it's likely that you are not going to feel so happy.

Another obstacle that prevents people from reconnecting with their inner child is all the negative things they experience in their lives. All the negative things that happen to us during the day can affect our ability to feel happy and relaxed.

For example, if you had a really bad day at work and you were told that you would be getting a large workload tomorrow, then it's likely that you will feel pretty stressed out about it. This can cause your mind to race and prevent you from feeling like yourself.

If you are feeling this way, you need to take some time out of your busy day to relax. Clear your mind of any thoughts that are causing you to worry or stress so you can finally feel like yourself again. It's the only way that you will be able to reconnect with your inner child and regain control of your life.

Another obstacle that many people face when they try to reconnect with their inner child is a lack of confidence in themselves. But there is no reason why you need to feel confident in order to reconnect with your inner child. In fact, most people aren't really capable of being confident in themselves because most of their confidence comes from external sources such as their family or others' opinions about them.

If you are experiencing this lack of confidence, think about things that help you feel good about yourself. One of the best ways to do this is to practice self-acceptance. If you are willing to accept yourself for who you are, then it's likely that other people will start to accept you for who you are as well.

Another obstacle that prevents people from reconnecting with their inner child is a lack of self-worth. If you don't have any self-worth, then you might not feel like you are good enough to be your own inner child. In fact, if you do have a low level of self-worth, then it's likely that every decision that you make will be based on how it makes other people feel about you.

The problem is, many people who suffer from low self-worth don't even realize it. They think they are doing the best that they can with their life. If your self-worth is low, you need to find ways to boost it. This will help you reconnect with your inner child.

Finally, one of the most common obstacles that prevent people from reconnecting with their inner child is simply the fact that they are afraid of letting go. For many, it's completely normal to feel like you can't let go because you are holding onto something very important inside your mind.

If you feel this way, it's important to understand what has kept you from letting go up until this point. It might be fear or it could be something else entirely. You need to understand what it is you are holding onto in order to move past this obstacle.

Letting go can be done in small steps until your mind is no longer afraid. Then you can begin the process of reconnecting with your inner child and becoming happier in your life.

The Dark Side of the Mind

If you are looking to reconnect with your inner child, then you are likely familiar with the concept of the "dark side" of our minds. Although this idea may sound somewhat strange, it's actually an important aspect of understanding why we function the way that we do.

Most people call this part of their mind their subconscious, but for purposes of understanding ourselves better, I like to think about it as my inner child. It's the part of me that never really grew up and still resides within my mind. It's the part of me that still has all the emotions and feelings a child would.

The reason why I like to think of myself as having an inner child is that it is a good way to explain why we sometimes do things that we don't really want to do. There are various reasons for this, but they mostly boil down to feeling like we have no choice in the matter.

For example, many people feel that they have no choice but to follow through with their responsibilities even if they don't want to. As a result, they find themselves stuck performing actions that can be extremely draining on their emotions.

The problem is, there are many people who have lost touch with their inner child and therefore are unable to understand why they are feeling so drained. They simply think that something is wrong with them or that they need to work harder at controlling their emotions.

But the truth is, it's not their fault. The reason why they feel like something is wrong with them is that they are unaware of their inner child and the effects it can have on them. They blame themselves for being weak when in fact, there is nothing wrong with them at all.

The reason why many people have a difficult time reconnecting with their inner child is that they are afraid of the "dark side" in themselves. They fear that if they let their inner child out, it will turn into a monster that could cause them to do things that they would never want to do.

There is also the belief that this part of ourselves is actually bad and therefore we shouldn't let it out. But if we don't let our inner child out, we will never really be happy. We need to open up and allow ourselves to connect with who we really are in order to move forward with our lives.

So if you have a fear of your inner child, understand that it's natural to be fearful. Most people who have a fear of their inner child don't really know what they are afraid of. They think the inner child something terrible when in fact, it can provide them with many benefits.

In the end, the only way to be free from this doubt is to become aware of your inner child and understand what it is all about. You can't really do this until you are willing to let it out to play. So if you are experiencing a hard time reconnecting with your inner child, then you may need to try and conquer your fears one day at a time.

Temptation and Attraction: There is a Way Around It

If you're experiencing difficulty reconnecting with your inner child then the problem could simply be that you're trying to do it from the wrong perspective. In other words, you're attracted to things of this world too much and as a result, you aren't able to let your inner child out.

There are many different ways to distract yourself, but one of the most common ways is by forming an attraction to someone. When you develop an attraction towards someone, you can forget about your own emotions and focus your attention on something else instead.

There are many different things that can cause you to be attracted to someone, including their physical appearance, personality, or even their financial status. It's normal for people to become attracted based on these three reasons alone, but the more important reason is the emotions that you feel inside of yourself.

When someone makes you feel emotions that are stronger than your own feelings of self-worth, it becomes extremely difficult to ignore these emotions.

But if you try and stay away from these emotions, then they will eventually go away on their own. In fact, many people have been able to erase the memories of certain periods in their lives simply by stopping themselves from thinking about it.

The reason why people have a hard time letting their inner child out is that they are going after things in their life that don't make them happy. It could be a new car or house or something else entirely.

If you are currently stuck on the material things of this world, then know that you aren't alone. Many people find themselves struggling to let their inner child out because they are too enthralled with the things around them. But in order to be happy, they have to put the things of this world aside so that they can be free.

Too many people are unable to do this because they are afraid of what might happen if they give up their material items. But this is just your mind trying to scare you into believing that there is no way for you to survive without these things. The truth is, if you are able to let go of these things, you will be able to gain some sort of happiness.

So while it may be tempting to keep reminding yourself that you can't live without your material items, don't do it. That's just your mind trying to keep you stuck in this world. Instead, remind yourself that you need to learn how to let go of the things of the world in order for you to gain happiness.

The best way for you to do this is to understand why it's so hard for people to let go of their material items. They are something that people are addicted to. If you are able to figure out the root of the problem, then you will be able to arrive at a solution that helps you let go of them.

You also have to define what you truly want in life. If you really want to be happy, you will need to make sure that what you are attached to is healthy. So think hard about what you want out of life and then make sure that it is good for you.

Once you've done this, then you'll be one step closer to truly understanding the difference between what you want vs. what your mind believes that you need to survive. This will give you the ability to look at all of your material items with a new perspective and make sure that they are actually helping you. If not, then it's time for them to go (or at some of them anyway).

If you are having a hard time letting go of your material items, I advise that you start living more simply. That way, you will be able to get used to not having these things around you. And if you are able to do that, you will be able to start focusing on the things in life that really matter.

Doing this is one of the best ways to become aware of your inner child and reconnect with it. You can't really do this until you are willing to detach yourself from your attachments.

CHAPTER 17: UNDERSTAND THE SPECIAL GIFT OF THE INNER CHILD

Your inner child has a special gift that only your deepest self knows about.

Your inner child is your childlike spirit. It is the part of you that allows you to enjoy life. It is what brings you joy. That special secret gift of your inner child is what makes your life worth living.

We must understand the secret gift of our inner child, so we can enjoy life to the fullest, so we can believe in magic and fairies again. To listen to your inner child is to listen to your heart. We all have an inner child who always wants us to love ourselves, so we can love others. It wants us to be happy and free!

To truly know yourself is to know what your secret gift is. The key is finding it. Uncover your secret gift by paying attention to yourself. You know it when you know it. You can't fake it. You can't make it up! It is not about what you do; it is only about who you are! Your inner child may seem like a little person, but rest assured, it is our heart!

We must understand and know what our secret gift is – and we can only do that by listening.

Our inner child wants us to be free and happy. We feel alone sometimes because we hide our gift from others. We feel like we don't fit in; we feel like we are different. We have a special gift but we can't show it, so we feel sad and ashamed.

Our inner child is a part of our heart that once knew what our secret gift was. But as we grew up, we disowned that wonderful person inside of us because it didn't fit into the world's definition of right and wrong.

We were told so many things that made us feel ashamed about ourselves. We were told many things about our inner child that made us feel alone. We were told what our inner child was not good at, so we disowned it. We became so busy with what society said that we forgot that inside of us there is a small child who wants the very best for us.

Know your secret gift – that is enough! Remember, you have to let yourself have fun, so you can believe in magic and fairies again! Don't let society put you down.

You can't fit in if you don't know what your secret gift is. You will only fit in when you learn to love, accept and be who you are supposed to be.

The way out is through your inner child. So let us go deep inside ourselves and find our inner child. Let us tell it that we will never abandon it again. Let us tell it that we will always be there for it. It is our heart. Our inner child knows the truth, no matter what happens. We must start listening to it once again!

Listen to Whatever Your Inner Child Has to Say

When we listen to our inner child, we are also listening to our heart. We are listening to what we truly need, want, and believe.

The inner child is a part of who we are. It's a little bit of ourselves that has been forgotten, taken for granted, or neglected by the self-conscious adult self.

Healing your inner child is not about forgetting the past. It's not about punishing yourself into thinking that you are "bad" or "terrible" inside. It's not about punishing your inner child for being a child, because children are wonderful.

It has to do with giving power back to the child within you. It's giving power back to your soul, giving it freedom, and letting it grow in its own way.

Letting the child in you be free, letting it play, and not burdening it with responsibilities that are not its own is how healing works best.

Your inner child has a voice. It's the voice of your emotions, your feelings, your sensations, and your sensations of inner safety.

If you listen to that voice, it will tell you what you need to hear.

You are listening to your inner child's voice when you are accepting all of your feelings, all of your thoughts, and all of your emotions. You are listening to that voice when you understand that these emotions are just passing sensations. They don't define you.

You listen to the voice in yourself when you don't pin it down with labels, because labels do not define who you are either. When you pin an experience or thought to a label, it becomes a "problem."

You listen to your inner child when you fully accept it for what it is. You listen to your inner child when you really allow yourself to feel and express every emotion and every reaction.

You listen to your inner child when you accept all of yourself, and don't try to control the situation. You listen to your inner child when you understand that some things are beyond your control.

You listen to your inner child when you understand that change is necessary. Change is inevitable, and it may be something you want for yourself, but it may not be something that will come quickly or easily.

Some people might feel that they don't have an inner child, that their life has been too hard, too difficult, or too painful to allow room for playfulness or innocence.

I know that you do.

Listen to your inner child's voice in the way that it speaks to you. Listen to what it needs you to hear, and listen in a way that supports its growth.

That is the way healing works.

Healing Doesn't Create New Wounds

Whether you have been trained to think that being a traumatized person is your fault, or whether you have been trained to think that being a traumatized person is a legitimate state of being, the truth is that traumatizing people do not have to stay traumatized.

Traumatizing people can heal themselves. They can heal from their experiences in order to be able to move on in healthy, loving ways.

It's really quite simple.

To get on with life, people need to heal from their experiences. In order to get on with life, they need to understand what they have experienced and how it has affected them.

Trauma is a natural response to unnatural experiences. "Unnatural" means that it wasn't something that was going to happen in the course of living a normal life. "Unnatural" means that you didn't understand what was going on, and it wasn't safe to remain in that state of being.

If you have been trained to think that being a traumatized person is your fault, it's time for you to heal from that concept. It's time for you to release yourself from the guilt and the shame of following the path of pain.

It's the right time for you to let go of what happened, so you can move forward with a newfound understanding and depth of self-confidence.

In order to get on with your life, it's necessary for you to move past the things that have been keeping you back from living a normal, healthy, and happy life. It's not about "letting go" of what happened in a destructive way. It's about understanding what has happened in a way that supports your growth and healing, so you can continue to live a happy and meaningful life.

Shame, guilt, and self-blame are not healthy ways of moving forward. Self-forgiveness is a much better way to free yourself from the past and allow yourself a future.

When you allow yourself to feel and express your emotions, and when you accept all of the thoughts which are coming into your mind, they lose power over you. You can't be scared of them anymore. You can't be afraid of the things that remind you of the past.

You will no longer allow yourself to feel trapped by pain.

You may still be sad about what has happened, but your sadness won't prevent you from living your life to the fullest. You may still feel angry about what has happened, but your anger won't prevent you from living your life to the fullest.

Thoughts and emotions are just passing sensations. Emotions aren't really things that you can control. You can control how you respond to them, but you can't necessarily control the feelings themselves.

You can feel sad, angry, or afraid of something without allowing those feelings to stop you from moving forward with your life.

That is the way life should be.

Feeling free from self-blame and self-forgiveness does take time. The first step is to understand that you are allowed to heal, and that you will heal, because you deserve to.

The second step is to release yourself from the concept that being a traumatized person is your fault.

You can't be a traumatized person and a happy person at the same time. You can't be a happy and a hurtful person at the same time.

There will always be an opportunity to heal, if you allow yourself to do so.

Bring Back the Joys of Childhood

There is a saying in psychology that most of our problems stem from childhood wounds. This is true because once they occur, they tend to go into our subconscious mind where they reside undetected until something triggers them later in life. These wounds can be caused by our family of origin, a broken relationship, a traumatic event, a natural disaster, a war, or an accident. Each of these events affects every part of our lives from the past to the present and continues on into our future.

The energetic, carefree days of childhood are a distant memory for many of us. We often fail to realize that one of the most powerful things we can do to heal ourselves is to bring back the joy of our early years. We are born pure, innocent, and joyful. We are not yet conditioned by the environment or societal norms, and our behavior is natural. As babies, we are in touch with our inner child. Our inner child is the true essence of who we are.

In our early years, we have the opportunity to live in a childlike state of being. Our inner child is pure and knows no fear or judgment. We do not yet understand that the world is a cruel place. We just know that life is full of wonder and happiness awaits us at every turn. When we were children, we spoke without thinking, ate without worry, played without inhibition, and became happy.

We spent time with people who loved us unconditionally, and we were loved in return. As children, we are naturally filled with love and happiness. But as adults, we have been conditioned to believe that we are inherently sad, depressed or frustrated.

The reason we become sad, anxious, or depressed is that we feel that something is wrong in our lives. Sadness and confusion begins to take over our thoughts and feelings.

We have been told lies about ourselves by others who have no idea what happiness is all about. They have never been given the gift of unconditional love, and they see themselves as flawed. We all have the innate ability to feel happy, but we must learn how to access that happiness from within. We can gain access to our inner child by reconnecting with our experience of being a happy child.

Think about a time or a place, a person, or an event that brought you happiness. These memories are here waiting for you to connect with them. They are part of your true self and they have been waiting to be healed from the scars of our past. As they heal, so will you.

There will be something new to learn always, so ask yourself if there is anything that would make you happier today than you were yesterday. If you are able to answer "yes," then begin experimenting with the behavior that would make you happier.

Simply take one step towards your goal of feeling happier. This is the beginning of healing yourself. As you continue this process, you will feel your happiness increasing each time you achieve one small goal. The key to releasing this happiness is to keep taking one step at a time until the goal is achieved.

By doing this simple exercise, you will be strengthening the "you" within yourself. The more you do this exercise, the more natural it will become. You will have access to your childlike state of being and you will then realize that happiness is a natural expression of who you are.

You can then pick up where that self left off and get to know these emotions in a new way.

We are meant to be happy, but we are not yet aware of how to access this happiness. Our lives have been filled with pain and confusion, so we need to understand that true happiness comes from the belief in oneself. It is up to every one of us to be the catalyst for our own happiness. Our lives are intended to be full of joy and wonder, and we need to stop believing that life is cruel. We are not victims, but deserving of happiness.

If you can imagine a time in your life when you felt happy, focus on the emotions you experienced. Take these emotions and put them into your present moment. Feel them as though they are happening now. Then you will begin to feel the energy of happiness flowing through your body with each breath you take. It is crucial to remember that all feelings are real and they can be experienced wherever we are at any given time.

Once you become aware of the energy of happiness, you will be able to bypass negative thoughts and emotions. As you learn how to do this, you will find yourself getting happier and more joyful as time goes on. You will quickly come to a certain point where your life is filled with happiness and wonder.

CHAPTER 18: 10 STRESS RELIEF STRATEGIES FROM YOUR INNER CHILD

By focusing on your inner child, you can begin to see how important it is to take care of yourself. When you learn to heal your inner child, you'll feel less stress and anxiety because you're learning how to listen to your emotions and feelings.

Here are the top 10 stress relief strategies from your inner child:

1. Daydreaming

If you're having problem sleeping at night, the repetitive nature of daydreaming may help get to the root of your stress. Once you get in touch with your inner child and focus on how it feels, daydreams can feel like a type of hypnosis. Daydreams can give you a sense of relief and relaxation.

2. Naps

It's very important to take some time for yourself when you're stressed out. The more you rush through your day without taking a break, the more stressed out you and your inner child will feel. Taking a nap can help your inner child recharge so it's able to function more naturally, and so you don't feel as though you need substances or other destructive behaviors to cope with stress.

3. Speaking Aloud

When your inner child is stressed out, being able to speak aloud can help you get in touch with what's going on inside of you. The more you're able to speak, the less your inner child may need to escape through substances or other behaviors. This will help you to feel more in control of your life.

- If you are unable to speak aloud, try writing down your thoughts and feelings. You can also draw what you are feeling through the use of art therapy.

- Try journaling about how it feels to be stressed out, but remember that writing doesn't have to be negative. It's important that you're able to express yourself, rather than keeping it all locked inside of you.

4. Pleasant thoughts

When you tell yourself positive affirmations, it's important to focus on what you want to accomplish. Avoid telling yourself things like "I can't do anything right." The more pleasant thoughts you have about who you are, the happier your inner child will be.

5. Exercise

If you're struggling with getting your inner child to calm down, there are plenty of physical activities that can help. Some people enjoy swimming, yoga, or even simple walking.

6. Being around other people

When you're stressed out, it's okay to lean on others for support. It's really important to remember that everyone haa their own problems and concerns, so try not to judge those who are struggling emotionally. Being around other people can help you get in touch with how you feel about yourself.

7. Taking care of your body

When you're stressed out, it's important to take care of your body. You might not feel like eating, but it will help reduce the amount of stress you're feeling. If you don't like eating, making an herbal tea can give your inner child something to drink that will help calm it down.

Train your inner child to accept emotional support from others by using positive affirmations.

8. Music

Listening to music can help your inner child to relax and feel less stressed. The more you're able to concentrate on the music instead of your internal conversations, the happier you will be.

9. Acceptance

When something is bothering you, it's essential to accept it and not run away from the feelings and emotions. When you can accept what is happening, it will help your inner child feel better about its current state of being.

10. Creativity

Being creative can help your inner child to feel relaxed. Creators tend to have a strong connection to their inner child, so they're able to take on its emotions and feelings without experiencing anger or frustration. This is why creative are able to create beautiful things that inspire others.

If you're having trouble dealing with stress, you don't have to suffer. You should reach out for emotional support because that's what your inner child needs to heal itself. Remember, our inner child is the key to our happiness, so be sure you are taking care of yours properly.

Working with Your Feelings

No matter your age, the feelings of childhood don't just go away. They'll always return, no matter how old you are. Learning to work with these emotions is an important step on the path of healing your inner child.

Most of us learned to ignore or even deny our feelings as children. We were taught that they weren't proper. That we shouldn't feel this way – and most of us got the message loud and clear.

But feelings are feelings. They are not something you should be ashamed of or laugh at. Feelings are an important part of who we are, just as much as the physical body is. It's up to us to remember them for what they really are – just another part of our selves.

Once we start learning to deal with them, we can move into a much healthier and happier place in our lives. We can be kids again without feeling that it is inappropriate. We can cry or get angry when we need to. We can recognize when our feelings are connected to an old issue in childhood and deal with it in a safe, healthy way.

Some people think that working with feelings is about dwelling on the past, but this isn't at all true. By working with our feelings, we are opening lines of communication that were previously blocked off. We are allowing the healing of our childhood wounds to take place in our adult lives. With this healing on an emotional level, we can put all of the old issues behind us and move forward with healthy emotional boundaries.

Our emotions are a part of who we are – they're a part of being human. When we feel, we're awake. We're not just a thinker or a doer at this point – we have feelings, and those feelings connect us to everything around us. The way that we deal with these feelings is an important part of our emotional development as children and as adults.

Your inner child needs you to teach it how to deal with its emotions properly so that you can heal from your childhood issues.

You may have always rejected these feelings, but they are still part of who you are. You may have suppressed them or denied them, but they still exist. It is time to take them out of the closet – it is time to stop hiding from them.

You need to create an emotional healing space in your life. This space is one where you can feel free to express yourself without fear or shame.

This doesn't mean that you will be overwhelmed by your emotions. It doesn't mean that you will break down in tears every day, or fly off the handle at every little thing – this isn't what an emotionally healthy life looks like once you've dealt with all of your past issues. Rather, it is the ability to express your emotions without guilt, without unnecessary pain and suffering – and the understanding that you are free to feel whatever you feel.

Being able to feel emotions is a great skill to have, and it's a skill that you need to teach your inner child.

As you move into your adult life, you can allow these feelings to be part of who you are. You can let them go and release them, and help your inner child finally release its anger.

Genuinely feeling your emotions can open a new life for you as you move forward into a healthier and happier future. It will change your life.

The Self-Destructive Inner Child

One of the biggest problems that people have with their inner child is that it has a tendency to sabotage the things in life they want most. For example, you might be in a romantic relationship with someone you really care about, but your inner child will often sabotage this relationship. It's not because you don't love this person anymore. Your inner child just doesn't know any better, because nobody has ever taught it how to love others or how to treat the people in your life with respect. Only you can teach your inner child this kind of behavior.

You might also be sabotaging your relationships with all of the people in your life because you don't think that these people are good enough for you. Your inner child might believe that you aren't good enough either, and it will do whatever it can to keep you from enjoying a healthy and fulfilling life.

In many cases, the reason why your inner child is acting in a self-destructive manner is because of pain from your past. You coped with this pain as a child by pulling away from the people who loved you the most, and now you're doing it again as an adult. Some people think they need to punish themselves for the things they did in the past, but this isn't true. Now is the time to heal your wounds and move on.

Your inner child could also be sabotaging your life because it wants you to be unhappy and displeased with yourself. If your inner child grew up with an absent parent or a parent that abused you in some way, then it's possible that you're experiencing these problems as an adult. Your inner child doesn't know how to be happy, because it never learned that feeling of happiness. When you want to be happy, you have to teach your inner child how to be happy. When you feel unhappy, try to find the reason why you're feeling this way. It's probably not something that will go away on its own. You have to tell your inner child that it has no right to make you feel this way – only you can decide which emotions are healthy for yourself and which aren't.

Your inner child could also be abusing you or giving you a bad name. If your inner child was hurt as a child, it might be sadistic and abusive because it doesn't know any better. The parents in their life didn't teach it how to love, and so this aspect of your personality has no idea how to express love in a healthy way. If you grew up with an abusive parent, you have to learn how to treat yourself and others in a very kind and loving way. Only you can teach your inner child that it deserves love from others.

It's very difficult to cope with a self-destructive inner child on your own. You may need professional help from a psychotherapist who specializes in this kind of problem. He or she can help you identify the things that are causing your inner child to act out in negative ways, and then help you to learn new ways of thinking and behaving that will bring peace and stability into your life.

Internalizing the problems of your inner child is a good way to make yourself feel miserable. This kind of self-hatred has to stop if you are to have any peace of mind. You can take control of your life by focusing on the positive things that happen. It's not easy, but it's possible.

The best way to help your inner child is by reconnecting with it. You can learn how to treat yourself better and stop hurting yourself by paying attention to your thoughts and feelings. The more you connect with your inner child, the more you'll be able to control it.

How the Inner Child Affects Your Self-Esteem

If you want to know how to develop your inner child, it's important to understand how low self-esteem can make you feel. If you don't feel great about yourself, it's impossible for you to take care of your needs or the needs of others. You need self-esteem in order to be effective as a human being. It's not possible for you to heal properly if your self-esteem is low.

Many people's self-esteem is low because they don't feel that they're good enough. They either feel that they did something bad or that the things that did happen were their own fault. This kind of thinking could make you feel bad about yourself, which makes it impossible for you to take care of your needs, but this doesn't have to be the case. What you have to do is learn how to get rid of negative thinking patterns so you are able to think about yourself in a more positive way. When you learn how to stop negative thinking, you can begin to build your self-esteem.

Give yourself some merit for the things you've been doing right in your life. If you're a good friend, a good son or daughter, a good spouse or partner, a loving parent, a hard-working person who is always trying to improve yourself and make your life better, then give yourself credit for all of these things. Give yourself credit, no matter what's going on in your life. Begin to notice the things that you're doing right. Make a list of your accomplishments and review it often. This can help you to feel good about who you are and what your life is like. You can't get depressed or sad if you've got lots of positive things going on in your life.

Focus on what you like about yourself instead of what you dislike. Instead of saying, 'I'm not good enough because I did this,' say, 'I'm good enough because I did this.' It's important to realize that you can do anything you want to. You can't do everything perfectly, but you can do everything extremely well. If you feel good about yourself, you will feel more confident and happy.

If someone has hurt or abused you, don't think of it as your own fault. People who abuse others are not good people – they are bad people who want to hurt others. It's important to realize that even if something bad has happened to you, it was not your fault. Take control of this scenario by learning to forgive yourself and heal from the wounds you've suffered.

You have a right to become happy, no matter what's going on in your life. If you're going through a rough time, it's important not to focus on what you think is wrong with the world and why things happen the way they do. Instead, focus on the good things in your life. To find the good in your life, look to your ac-complishments and use them as inspiration for what you want to do next. Instead of thinking that you have no control over your life, realize that you are in complete control of your own destiny. When you learn how to give yourself credit for all the things that are going well in your life, it will be much easier to deal with anything negative that comes along.

CHAPTER 19: A NEW WORLDVIEW

When the healing process is over, you should feel a sense of relief and accomplishment. All of the stress and pressure has been released from your body, mind, and energy levels. You can now go back to your daily routine without any worries or concerns. The best way to go about the healing process is to enjoy it. Concentrate on relaxing and letting your body and mind be free of all the stress that you're feeling. It is the healing process that will help you to understand that you are capable of dealing with all of your problems, issues, or fears. You are stronger than you believe. Trust yourself and know that you can heal.

You should feel comfortable with the fact that any physical or emotional problems that you had in the past are disappearing from your body. Know you will be able to overcome any issues or fears or problems in your life after you have completed this process. You can continue growing and learning more about yourself every day, every moment. Recognize that you can handle all of the challenges that life has in store for you.

Integrate the lessons and insights from the healing process into your daily life. All of the issues and concerns that you have had in your past will be gone forever. You'll see a complete change in your attitude and outlook on life as a result of this healing process. It will help you to become a happier, healthier, and stronger person.

The best way to take care of your body and mind after the healing process is to make sure that you stay physically fit and healthy. Do all you can to help your body recover from any physical or emotional problems that you had. Exercise often and eat healthy foods. Do all that you can to start feeling healthier and happier than ever before.

You should also try to develop your self-confidence. All of the wisdom and knowledge that you have gained from this healing process will provide you with the strength and courage to over-come any challenges that life has in store for you. You will be able to grow through every challenge that life puts before you. Once you go through the healing process, you'll know that you are strong enough to conquer anything.

Achieving Enlightenment and a New World View

The enlightenment process is an advanced spiritual healing method that can take you beyond the ordinary level of being to a higher state of being that is filled with peace, joy, love, and harmony. This process allows you to experience life on a much deeper level. This process can help you achieve enlightenment and create profound changes in your daily life.

The enlightenment process allows you to "let go" of all of the stresses in your life. At the same time, it lets you to release your fears and doubts. It helps you to relax and to open up and accept the positive change that is happening in your life.

This can be used to heal any negative thoughts, feelings, or emotions that you might be experiencing. This process allows you to let go of all of the burdens in your life so that you can start living life with a true sense of happiness.

When you learn how to use the enlightenment process, it will be easier for you to recognize the problems and concerns that you have in life. You'll be able to identify what your problems or concerns are and how they affect your day-to-day life. This will allow you to deal with your problems and concerns in a more positive way.

You'll be able to see how each of your issues and challenges affect your self-esteem, self-confidence, and the way that you think about yourself and the people around you. You'll learn to understand yourself and others a lot better as a result of learning this process.

You may use this process to improve any relationships with friends, family, or others. You can use this process to heal all of your family problems, issues, or fears. You can use this transcendental spiritual method of healing to help every member of your family feel healthier and happier.

The enlightenment process is an extremely powerful healing technique that can help you to create profound changes in your life. It will help you to achieve the goals that you have always wanted to achieve. It will release your inner potential and allow you to enjoy a new level of living and being. It will help you to experience a higher state of health and wellbeing.

This process helps you to mentally, emotionally, and physically move forward so you can start accomplishing the things that are most important to you. You don't have to allow negative thoughts or emotions or doubts or fears to stop you anymore. When you learn how to use this process, you can move forward with your life, regardless of what might be happening around you.

This process can help you reach a new level in your life. It will help you to open yourself up in a way that will allow you to experience a whole new level of being.

The enlightenment process is perfect for people that have problems with their relationships or who have difficulty in life in any other way. You can use this process to improve all of your relationships with others, whether they are personal, romantic, professional, or familial. Your relationship with God can also be improved as a result of this process.

When you learn how to use the enlightenment process, you'll be able to achieve a sense of detachment from the problems of life. You'll be able to perceive your life from a higher perspective. This will allow you to let go of negative thoughts, feelings, and emotions. It will allow you to release any fears that you have been experiencing.

This method of healing allows you to recognize that everything that happens in your life is meant for your highest good and for the highest good of everyone else in your life. It helps you to see how the problems and challenges that you're experiencing are meant to prepare you for a new level of being. It gives you a more advanced spiritual understanding so that you can more easily discern and recognize the problems and challenges that you're experiencing.

This method of healing allows you to experience fearlessness and freedom from worry and stress. It helps you to know that everything that happens in your life is for your highest good. When you learn how to use this method, it will allow you to move forward with your life.

Leaving Your Past behind You and Moving Forward Through the Transitional Process

Our childhood may cause us to feel anger, bitterness, resentment, sorrow, sadness or fear. These are understandable emotions because of the hurtful stories we were told about ourselves by our parents. Our childhood experience may have taught us that we didn't have any worth or value as a child. We must learn that this is not true. We were indeed special to our parents. Our parents told us this by the way they behaved toward us. But we learned not to trust our own feelings; we learned not to trust ourselves.

Leaving your past behind you and moving forward through the transitional process is the most important part in the healing process. You must explore your past. You must understand it fully. You must understand your parents' behavior toward you and the extent to which they either caused or supported your growth.

Allow yourself to feel the feelings that are associated with these early memories. When you are not afraid of these feelings, they can be very helpful in the healing process. Remember, it is the emotion itself that heals. It is not about what happened to you or how you felt at the time. It is about what has happened to you since then and how you have healed. You healed your inner child when you learned how to nurture yourself and take care of yourself.

Learn to look at the positive aspects of your childhood. Forgive your parents for their mistakes in raising you. Understand that in most cases their actions were in response to their own wounds in life; they did not know any better way to raise a child. Before you can live in the present moment, you must be able to forgive. You must be able to forgive your parents for their mistakes in raising you. You must be able to forgive yourself for the mistakes you have made in your own life. You can do this when you are willing to accept responsibility for the choices you have made. Let go of any blame, anger, resentment or hatred toward others, including your parents. Once you can do this, you will find that you have a new freedom – a freedom from the old guilt and shame, a freedom from all of the old conditioned fears. And YOU WILL BE YOU. You will finally be able to live life at your own pace. You will no longer have to prove anything to anyone or hide parts of yourself so deeply that they are not even accessible to yourself. You will be able to reveal all of your parts to yourself...all of them... without fear. You will no longer be afraid to be "on stage" on any level of your life. You will finally be able to trust yourself without concern for who is watching or what the consequences might be. You will finally be able to live with integrity, truth and compassion without fear of losing the approval of others. You will be able to take responsibility for all of your actions and decisions without feeling regret, shame, guilt or remorse. These are the characteristics of an adult. There is no fear in an adult: no self-doubt, no self-criticism and no self-recrimination. There is no fear of being found out, no fear of being seen as too much, no fear of being inadequate. When you are an adult, you will no longer judge yourself or others. There will be no need for self-sacrifice because you understand how to love others without diminishing yourself. You know how to love others without stopping the flow of your own life. Truth and freedom from the old judgments are natural components of growing into an adult. Until you have lived this for yourself, it is impossible to understand the emotional freedom that comes at this level.

Many people are stuck in their old stories because they are not willing to release them to move forward with their life. They are afraid to reach out for love, because they are still holding on to the stories that have trapped them in shame, guilt and fear. They are afraid to move forward because they are afraid of what life will bring. They are still living in the past and not enjoying their present. They do not understand that the past is over and they have nothing to fear from it anymore. It is very important to understand this: It is NOT what happened to you, but what has happened since then that defines who you are today.

What happened in your childhood is done and cannot be changed. You cannot change what you did back then – it is gone forever. What you can change is who you are today and where you are going. It is important to understand that the past only controls the present as long as we continue to feed it with our old stories and parts of ourselves.

CONCLUSION

Your past might be painful but your present does not have to be. Tapping into your inner child can be a great source of healing and personal growth. Reframe the past as an experience that made you stronger, gave you compassion for others and created space for new perspectives on life.

Do not take it upon yourself to change the past. No matter how much you want to blame your parents, blame yourself or blame someone else, it will not change anything. Blaming leads nowhere but to more pain and suffering for you and others. Only in accepting the past and consciously surrendering to the present moment can you really begin to heal.

Your inner child can be healed by letting it go. You can heal the wounded child by surrendering to the present moment, accepting its presence, suspending judgment of it and loving it unconditionally. As you heal your inner child, you will be less reactive to dependency, fear and anger. As you heal you will also be able to better care for yourself and others. You will feel more secure, happy and whole.

Your wounds can still affect your present but as long as your inner child is not healed, they will continue to control your life. Such wounds can be healed by allowing them to move through you without holding onto them or their pain. You can heal your inner child by loving yourself unconditionally.

Your past is in you, but it does not define you. You can release the past and move forward in your life with love and compassion for yourself and others. You can heal your inner child by simultaneously grieving the loss of your past while creating a new story for who you are now.

Your inner child has an agenda that must be dealt with if you want to heal it. Such wounds are usually the result of unresolved issues from your childhood. You must address them if you want to be free of them. You can begin to heal your inner child by letting go of the past and surrendering unconditionally to the present moment.

Your inner child is not complete without its core wound. Core wounds are usually the result of events that happened to you as a child that shut down your ability to mature and grow into a healthy self-efficacy. By resolving such core issues, you can begin to heal your inner child so it stops controlling your life.

The wounds of your past have a purpose for you. By healing them, you will gain a more complete self and be able to live more authentically and honestly with yourself and others. You can heal your inner child by releasing the pain from them and allowing new perspectives on the past.

You have been conditioned to react from a place of fear, insecurity or dependency on others. As you heal your inner child, these reactions can be altered through unconditional self-love.

In this book you have been introduced to the concept of your inner child. As you read through these pages, you began to learn about this dynamic part of yourself.

Your inner child is not a problem to be solved. It is a dynamic part of who you are that can be healed. When you heal your inner child, your perspective on the world will change. You will be more open, loving and compassionate. You will also feel less insecure, fearful or needy.

Your inner child is not who you really are. It is only one part of who you are that has not been healed. Healing this part of yourself can allow other parts to become more healthy and whole. Be gentle with yourself while you learn how to heal your inner child while still maintaining control over who you are in the present moment.

Your journey through this book has been for growth and change, not punishment or guilt. Do not struggle against your inner child any longer. As you begin to heal it, accept that everything in life happens for a reason.

Thank you for reading this book. I hope that if you have been on a similar journey as we have presented here, you will find healing and growth within yourself.

www.ingramcontent.com/pod-product-compliance
Lightning Source LLC
Chambersburg PA
CBHW061250120726
48001CB00001B/241